Table of Contents

This book is designed to provide accurate and authoritative information on the subject of personal finances and real estate investing. While all of the stories and anecdotes described in the book are based on true experiences, most of the names are pseudonyms, some stories are compilations, and some situations have been changed slightly for educational purposes and to protect each individual's privacy. It is sold with the understanding that neither the Author no the Publisher is engaged in rendering legal, accounting, investing or other professional services by publishing this book. As each individual situation is unique, questions relevant to personal finances and specific to the individual should be addressed to an appropriate professional to ensure that the situation has been evaluated carefully and appropriately. The Author and Publisher specifically disclaim any liability, loss, or risk that is incurred as a consequence, directly or indirectly, of the use and application of any of the contents of this work.

ISBN – 13: 978-1456472573

Why Florida and Why Now

Canadians are typically conservative when it comes to investing – just look at how our banks managed themselves during the recent financial crisis. They came away fairly unscathed on a world scale because of their conservative practices and stringent lending practices. Many Canadians have never seen 0% down payment mortgages and loans, like Americans saw in the past decade.

When the USA real estate market collapsed for the first time in history in 2007 for the most powerful nation on earth, everyone took notice. I mean everyone in every country was watching since the world economies are now more inter-dependent from exports and imports to currency fluctuations, than ever before. Everyone was asking whether apocalypse was upon us, or whether the end of the world economic order, as we knew it, was here. It was scary but it kept getting scarier day by day. Large institutional investment banks like Bear Stearns folded and so did Lehman Brothers, then GM, Chrysler and possibly Ford were going to fold, as the Government was trying to catch up to what was going on. The enormity of the shenanigans that were going on in the financial markets totally side swiped the Government.

I had stocks and ETFs and I was glued to the financial networks all day long, hungry for information and then more information. It became an obsession. I'm sure others were doing the same as they worried about their pensions, RRSPs and their jobs since Canada depends on the USA for exports.

Jobs were disappearing in the USA at an alarming rate. Companies were protecting themselves and dumping employees like you'd drop a stock when the market starts tanking. There was nowhere to hide; stocks for good companies (Dell, HP, GE) were getting hammered and valuations were getting cut in half. Bonds, treasury bills and housing prices were dropping like a stone. Commodities like gold and silver were also dropping. Everyone was going into cash! People felt another Depression was coming similar to 1929 where cash was king; and everyone was going into cash or just staying put - hoping this would correct and blow over. Financial advisors were not calling their clients because nobody had answers, or at least any good ones.

I purchased real estate in the past, back in 1989, when the peak of the Canadian market was near the top. I learned a very important lesson; Lesson No. 1 - never buy high and sell low again. I bought a house for $210,000 and sold it 4 years later for $180,000. Had I held onto that property for another 10-15 years, I could have almost doubled my investment. The house today would be worth close to $400,000, and in Toronto that's close to the average home price today. Another financial lesson learned; Lesson No. 2 - learn the cycles of different investment instruments and come in at the right time (refer back to Lesson No.1 if you don't know). Everything works in cycles, a natural rhythm of ebbs and flows, peaks and valleys, over-heated and cooling, rallys and corrections. If you find yourself in a valley, cooling cycle or a correction - have patience, that's Lesson No. 3.

I suppose I felt the sting of losing money pretty hard and therefore stayed out of real estate investments for a while. Instead, I put my money into stocks. My judgment and timing couldn't have been worse. I got hit in the Dot.com bubble which happened in 1999. I lost close to 50% of my holdings (remember lesson # 1). I was impatient and sold my holdings to get out (remember Lesson No. 3).

When the Financial Crisis of 2007 happened, I had to ask myself, is this it? Is this my time? Do I go for it? After all, Warren Buffet was the guy that said when somebody yells fire and everyone is running for the exit, you should be choosing your seat for the next show, because there always is one (Lesson No. 1 and 2).

I listened to the news, and saw that the Government pumped in money to hold steady companies like AIG, GM, Chrysler, Bank of America, JP Morgan Chase, the list goes on. This told me that the United States was acting responsibly. It wanted to do everything to avoid default. Yes, it was going to take on a huge debt, but it did not want to devalue its currency like Brazil or Argentina did in the past. In a certain way, they were acting like a Canadian would. Canadians will fight to the death to avoid a bankruptcy claim against their credit rating.

So what do I do? The dollar was at par with the US dollar, house prices have dropped about 50% and looks to be still dropping, is this a good time to go in? I needed someone that could counsel me.

There are plenty of Real Estate Agents and Brokers that can help you with purchasing Florida Real Estate from either side of the border. However, I was looking for more advice and coaching than just from a Real Estate Agent.

The person I had questions for would be someone who

- was a Real Estate Agent familiar with USA and specifically Florida Real Estate; especially one who worked with Canadians;
- but I also had questions for a Real Estate Lawyer, and ;
- questions for someone that owned property in Florida and wanted to know how they rent to locals;
- I also had questions for someone that was experienced in renting vacation rentals or vacation homes.

Actually, I was looking for someone that had all these experiences and if that person was a Canadian, then I would be totally happy. That was a tall order. I needed a coach and advisor that would perform the role of consultant to me. I would have paid that person for this service.

I was beginning to realize during my search that everyone had their specialty and expertise, and of course, motive to sell their product or service, but nobody that could pull it all together for me. I would be asking numerous people in phone conversations or over the internet in blogs the following questions.

1. **What are the implications of investing in Real Estate cross border?**

2. **Is now the right time to invest or should I wait a few more years?**

3. **What areas should I be looking at where quality of life is good and rentals are in demand?**

4. **When could I realistically expect values to come back to those in 2005, when they were at their peak?**

5. **Should I invest in Gated Communities, Condos, Single family homes or just Land?**

6. **What are the hidden costs that you uncover over time or at time of purchase?**

7. **What tax laws are at play and should I invest as an individual or should I setup a corporation?**

8. **What are my rights as a landlord and how do I get great tenants or handle them if they're not?**

9. **How can I manage a remote property 2500 kilometers away, would I need anyone to help me?**

10. **Should I rent my property as an Annual Rental or as a Vacation Rental and can I use it myself for vacations?**

I never found the magical person who could help me out but the Internet had so much information and abundant tools to help me, I eventually gained enough knowledge to proceed in making up my own mind using my own judgment with a healthy level of common sense (for those married men, that means your wife).

This book was written for those needing that Consultant. I don't have an angle or a product to sell you other than information, which is all within this book. I tell you what I did and how I reached that decision, but I don't try to corner you into one solution or the other. I am your Consultant, Coach, Advisor to help you with your own questions. I know that I would have appreciated a digest of information that I'm about to give you with tools, techniques, information and straightforward advice that will help you decide whether this is the right investment for you.

Some other areas that I'll be able to share my experiences with you are to:

- **Provide you with a Financial Analysis tool I created on Google Docs, to see if the property can be a cash flow positive investment. It also shows you all the other expenses you need to consider as part of your decision.**

- **Show you how I manage my properties remotely, which will save you time and expense of having a Property Management company (on average they take 20% of your rent). I manage 4 properties remotely today.**

- **Show you how to advertise your properties (for free), screen potential tenants, perform credit checks on prospective tenants and furnish you will all the forms you'll need as a Landlord to setup Leases.**

- **Provide you with an online tool to have prospective tenants submit their interest in your property to you. The tool asks them for info and sends it to you automatically. It helps you decide whether they are a good fit.**

- **Provide you with tools to see your property from 2500 kms away, including Google Street Maps but also get access to Municipal records that will give you data on taxes, sales history and pictures of your investment.**

- **Also provide you with an online Google tool that will help you track your expenses and at the same time have it ready for your tax form submissions at tax time. One mouse click will print it out for your tax accountant.**

- **Show you how to advertise your investment as a Vacation Rental for as little as $99/year to see if it would attract potential vacationers. This basically would be your market research to analyze the potential.**

My experience with some bad investment choices gave me the lessons I needed to learn to capture this moment in time. This time I was not part of the crash or held any USA real estate investments. It was a perfect storm with the currency being close to par with the US dollar and where real estate prices collapsed to bargain basement prices.

I learned over time that stocks can disappear entirely. Look at Nortel and those poor Canadians that held so much stock in this technology darling. Companies can be corrupt or badly managed, like Nortel was, and that is something you don't have complete visibility to as a stock holder. You could wake up one day to the news about how your stock tumbled 75% overnight because of SEC investigations into corruption or foul play; no thank you.

I learned that real estate always has value. It may go up or down, but for the most part, it will trend upwards if you come in low enough, like now. Lesson No. 4 for me was that you make your real estate profits on the *buy* and not the *sell* portion of your investment. The reason that it always holds value is because it has a basic functional purpose. People need homes to live in – you can rent it. People will also always need a vacation and as resorts and hotel prices continually rise, vacation homes will always have a place for large families taking vacation.

I wanted control of my investment - something I could manage and improve upon with upgrades if I wanted to.

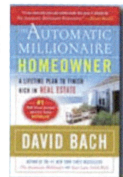

I also decided that owning Florida real estate could be used by my family and friends as a vacation home or a retirement destination as a snowbird someday or as a vacation rental if I'm looking for a retirement income stream. It just appealed to me on so many different levels that I said I could not overlook this opportunity - should I say it - of a lifetime.

This book is going to give you plenty of information. At times it may read like an Owner's Manual on how to invest and manage it from a distance, but that's what I would have wanted to know when I was looking. I share with you the tricks, techniques and tools I used to search for; buy and manage my investment.

There are basically 10 reasons why I decided to buy my first house in Florida in 2008, then my 2nd and 3rd home in 2009 (via Internet only) and my 4th home in 2010 (via the Internet). I list them in priority sequence on the following pages.

I'll warn you now. Once you experience your first real estate purchase in the sunshine state, you'll want to do it again, and possibly again.

Remember, I'm not selling a new idea here. Just read any of David Bach's books, like the Automatic Millionaire HomeOwner or Robert Shemin's books on real estate as viable ways to wealth.

http://www.finishrich.com/books/automaticHO_brandhome.php

http://www.getrichwithrobert.com/

10 Reasons that made me Invest

1. Personal Tax Write-off

Americans get to deduct their mortgage interest from their Federal government through the IRS (Internal Revenue Service). Wouldn't you like that same privilege? Well, as an investor, you actually get that same privilege plus many more tax advantages. The difference is that you file your tax return for this investment with Canada Revenue Agency (CRA) and deduct the investment expenses, like Mortgage Interest from your taxable income thereby reducing your taxable income before Federal and Provincial taxes owing are calculated.

It doesn't matter whether you have a USA mortgage or a Canadian Mortgage, or whether you bought this house with just an Equity Line of Credit (ELOC). As long as you can show that you paid interest on the investment, you are eligible to claim this as an investment expense. I highly recommend you get a tax accountant to help you with filing taxes, but remember, their fees are also tax deductible.

As an investor, you actually get to deduct more than Interest on the money borrowed to buy the property, you get to deduct Advertising, Maintenance costs, Repairs, Professional Service fees like Lawn Mowing or Pool service, Property Management and even Travel Expenses (within reason) to visit your property once a year to perform inspections on your investment and meet your tenants.

My point here is that you actually have more benefits over a USA Home owner who gets to deduct their mortgage interest while living in their home. I dedicate a whole section to Taxes and what you are required to file in the USA with the IRS, so I won't elaborate any further here.

My motive for buying Florida Real Estate was always from an Investor standpoint. It's great to make lots of income but keeping as much of it and sheltering it from tax is perhaps even more important. If you earn $85,000 per year for example, then you will pay 26% federal tax plus another 11.16% provincial tax (2009 rate table for Ontario). You've just handed over 37.16% of your money to support healthcare, roads and infrastructure to Canada.

What is the moral of this story? As a high income earner, you want to reduce your taxable income. You can do this with RRSP contributions (up to a limit) and with investment expenses (no limit) like Florida property. Those are just two examples.

Another area of write-off is the annual trip you are allowed to claim for visiting your property in Florida or meeting your tenants to perform repairs or to perform upgrades to the property. These are expenses you are allowed to claim in order to manage your investment. That doesn't mean you can claim your golfing green fees or cruises you take while down there. However, transportation, meals and lodging are reasonable expenses.

2. Unprecedented Real Estate Crash

We have never in our lifetime seen such fallout from extreme highs in American Real Estate. Although the "American Dream" meant different things to different people it was basically "an urge to live a better life" and for the largest investment most Americans make, this meant owning real estate. Most Americans saw their real estate values continually go in one direction since World War II, and that was up.

Most Americans that I spoke with over the years had many homes. The reason was simple. If American real estate only increases in value every year, why not have many homes that increase in value to provide a multiplier effect. This was essentially a good financial strategy up until 2007. For many, it was their retirement plan. For others that had slightly less financial discipline, it was a means to re-finance their home as it appreciated in value so that they could buy more cars, send their kids to the best colleges or just take extravagant vacations.

Mortgage Brokers were writing up mortgages to those that could not afford homes with as little as 0% down payment and very low initial interest rates that were set to pop after a few years. Borrowers were not concerned because they "knew" that they could sell that home in a few years if the mortgage became unaffordable for a substantial gain. Two of the largest Mortgage underwriters were Fannie Mae and Freddie Mac. Brokers were paid handsome commissions for bringing Fannie and Freddie as many mortgages possible. The problem was when these mortgage brokers started making huge sums of money and became "*motivated*" to put through as many Loans possible without checking to see if the borrower could pay the loan. These are now referred to as "Liar Loans". These were essentially low quality, bad loans (sub-prime).

Wall Street got wind of these subprime loans and thought they could create a new Security to sell called a CDO (Collateralized Debt Obligation). What they would do is package up 100 of these bad loans and sell them to their Institutional Investors. When the Home Owners with mortgages started to default on their payments, after rates jumped up after a couple of years, as part of their mortgage contract, the house of cards started to fall for these Institutional Investors, like Bear Stearns and Lehman Brothers. Click this link below for a candid and poignant slide show explanation of how the mortgage meltdown happened.

http://www.slideshare.net/MrSold/Presentation1-1044602

So why Invest in Florida? Prices of USA Real Estate have fallen as much as 70% in some states. Those states most affected were Arizona (Phoenix), Nevada (Las Vegas) and Florida. I chose Florida because of:

- Boating – with access to Water (Gulf of Mexico, Atlantic Ocean)

- Golf – some of the best courses available to avid golfers

- Beaches – some of the best white sand beaches in the world

- Tourism – International Tourists, 5 Major cruise ports, Disney World

- Shopping – major outlets and malls

- Cities – from flashy Miami to seaside resorts (Destin, Tampa, Naples, Fort Myers Beach, Key West) with great International access across major Airports (Miami - MIA, Orlando - MCO, Tampa - TPA, Fort Myers - RSW)

Most of us know that Florida is known as a Retirement State. Most of us also know that the first phase of the Baby Boomers is due out this year in 2010. Where will they go? Well, there's lots of conflicting research on that, some say Costa Rica, but that country has already seen massive price increases. Some say Mexico but you need to be careful in a country with such corruption and violence with massive drug cartels. Some think Central America but if Spanish isn't your main language, you need to be careful about where you wonder.

Americans are loved most in America and Canadians are welcomed as we almost share a similar culture and language. We probably watch more American television channels that Canadian channels.

Compare Florida price per square foot and you'll quickly see that you get more real estate per square foot value for anything else. Just check out http://www.zillow.com and http://www.realtytrac.com.

You can find a property for less than $25 / sq ft where in other markets that same house will cost $500+ / sq ft. I have seen single family homes  with a pool go for what you would pay for a brand new 2011 Ford Edge ($35,000) and has over 2,000 sq ft of living space (pictures of this house located in Cape Coral are shown on right side of this page – MLS number 201043673). Actually the car was a little more expensive after taxes and options.

The time is ripe for investing, whether it's Florida or a place in California.

Most of the downside risk of price drops has already been absorbed. The price may go sideways for a few more years, but in the end, Real Estate has always been a tangible asset. So why invest in Florida? If prices don't increase even for 10 years, this is an asset that can generate cash as a Vacation Rental or Annual Rental (consider it as your Dividend if you were to hold a stock) or you can go enjoy it yourself. As the great investor Warren Buffet wrote, "Never invest in anything you don't understand".

3. American Renter Population has Increased Substantially

More Americans than ever before are again becoming a renter nation due to the barrage of home Short Sales, Foreclosures and business bankruptcies that are occurring which now represent about 33% of the population and is predicted to go to 40%. http://www.jchs.harvard.edu/publications/rental/rh06_americas_rental_housing.pdf.

This is good news for Landlords looking for tenants. When I posted my homes for rent, the biggest challenge for me was trying to sift through the number of interested inquiries. I developed an automated system which I describe later in this book on how best to handle this.

Many Americans have damaged credit scores as a result of losing their homes into Foreclosure, where the bank repossesses the home and resells it on the open market. Banks will not lend to those with subpar credit scores because they are very risk averse after the Sub-prime collapse and after the Financial Reform Bill in 2010. That leaves these folks looking for a rental.

Would I rent to someone that has a subpar Credit Score or went into Bankruptcy? Yes, I would and already have, but it all depends on their situation. Put yourself in their shoes. Imagine if you moved up to a larger home a few years ago and paid $500,000 for it and your Mortgage was for $400,000 (20% down payment) and the market cratered making your house now worth $250,000. You are now paying a mortgage for a house that was worth twice as much as what the market price dictates. The Mortgage Meltdown brought everyone's home price down. That's unfair, but it's reality. I don't discredit those innocent bystanders.

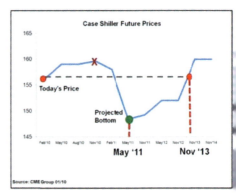

Some folks are just walking away from their debt obligation because they feel that going bankrupt will be cleared from your record before their house value goes back up to what it was. Besides, many might have as low as 3% down payment that they are walking away from, so they didn't lose much. Instead, they'll rent, save their money and wait until the time is right for them to reinvest into a home, if ever.

For more information about what is projected for the USA rental market and home prices (which are predicted to bottom in May 2011 as shown by Case Schiller chart above) refer to the Naked Capitalism website:

http://www.nakedcapitalism.com/2010/04/guest-post-rental-prices-up-or-down.html

4. Weakness in US Dollar

When I bought my first home in 2008, the Canadian dollar was at par with the greenback. Just a month before that time, the Canadian dollar was actually worth more than the USD for a brief period. It then retreated over the last few years back closer to .90 cents but then in 2010 when I purchased my 4th home, it was at .99 cents Canadian for 1 US Dollar which influenced part of my purchase decision.

If the USD becomes strong again against world currencies, then the parity will widen and it will become more expensive to buy American real estate. If you invest now, your investment gets that currency increase in value, when you sell. Do I think USD will go back up? Yes, I do. The USA is still the World superpower nation. Some economists think China poses a serious threat but China would need to triple its GDP numbers in order to take the leading position.

The USA is about 10 times the size of Canada in terms of its GDP growth and population. It's not a stretch to imagine that this world superpower will reinvent itself and learn from its mistakes going forward. A new generation of workers devoted to Clean Energy companies, Silicon Valley software projects like Web 3.0, advanced Healthcare and Pharmaceutical breakthroughs could bring this super power back its glory days.

Rank	Country	GDP (millions of USD)
1	United States	14,256,275
2	Japan	5,068,059
3	People's Republic of China	4,908,982
4	Germany	3,352,742
5	France	2,675,951
6	United Kingdom	2,183,607
7	Italy	2,118,264
8	Brazil	1,574,039
9	Spain	1,464,040
10	Canada	1,336,427
11	India	1,235,975
12	Russia	1,229,227
13	Australia	997,201
14	Mexico	874,903

This will take several years but in the meantime, you should take advantage of this perfect storm where house prices are low and the Canadian currency is comparatively high.

5. Tourism

Florida gets about 80 Million visitors to the Sunshine State every year. In 2009 that figure was down by almost 1%, in part due to the economy. In 2010 it was down due to the oil spill creating doubt about beach access.

- Florida has 19 commercial airports (12 international) across the entire panhandle state

- Florida has 5 major cruise ports, 1200 miles of sand beach and over 1250 Golf Courses

- Florida Everglades, Disney World, Kennedy Space Center, Beaches, Boating, Fishing, Golfing, Wildlife, Parks, Lighthouses all provide for interesting vacation destinations.

- Miami, West Palm Beach, Ft. Lauderdale, Naples, Tampa, Key West all provide high end shopping destinations (1-2 hours drive from each other on average). State tax is 6%.

- Number of people who move to Florida each day is 1,000 / day.

For more information visit the following link:

http://www.stateofflorida.com/Portal/DesktopDefault.aspx?tabid=95

6. Language and Culture

The South of Florida, particularly Miami is growing in population from many Latino based countries (Mexico, Puerto Rico, Central America and South America) and therefore has a large Spanish language preference. Colombians, who often call Miami the most beautiful city in their country, has always been drawn to Florida. The difference now is the upside-down economics. It is cheaper to buy in Miami than in Bogota, and you can fly between the two cities for $59 each way. For facts on Florida culture and language visit:

http://en.wikipedia.org/wiki/Florida

Based on my experience, the East coast (Miami, Fort Lauderdale, and West Palm Beach) will have many people that come from the North East USA (New York, New Jersey, Connecticut, North Carolina) as well as Canadian and Europeans owning vacation or rental properties there. The West coast (Tampa, Sarasota, Fort Myers, Bonita Springs, and Naples) will have a slightly slower pace than the East coast and will have many people from the mid-west United States (Ohio, Pennsylvania), Canadians and Germans.

7. Weather

Although Florida is known around the world for its balmy weather and called the "Sunshine State", it actually ranks as number 6 behind 5 other states (Arizona, California, Nevada, New Mexico and Texas). Florida still gets its fair share of sun. Key West sees sun an average 76% of its available daylight hours, followed by Miami with 70%. South Florida is consistently warmer than anywhere else in the continental United States, and have more days with sun accompanied by 20%-70% cloud cover than anywhere else.

The state's mild winters have made it a haven for retirees. Summers can be long and hot with showers providing much appreciated relief during the rainy season. Coastal areas also experience gentle breezes during the summer.

Summer	Winter
80.5 (F) degrees (26.9 C) (North Florida)	53.0 (F) degrees (11.7 C) (North Florida)
82.7 (F) degrees (28.2 C) (South Florida)	68.5 (F) degrees (20.3 C) (South Florida)

In terms of Hurricanes, Florida's hurricane season is from June 1 - November 30. This happens to also be the hottest and most humid times to be down there and is also known as their rain season. The rains come almost daily but last sometimes only minutes. The lightning that will sometimes accompany these showers provide for a phenomenal light show and are magnificent to watch from a safe distance. Full hurricane information can be found at the following web address: http://www.nhc.noaa.gov/

The homes I bought are all located in the South-West region of Florida called Cape Coral. Since most Hurricanes come from the Atlantic going east, they usually turn north up along the Eastern coast (South/North Carolina) or they head straight into the Gulf of Mexico and go north into Texas, Louisiana as Katrina did. They rarely do what Hurricane Charley did in 2004, which was go into the Gulf and then turn North and Eastward going straight across the Panhandle as shown in the picture. Charley hit Punta Gorda which is just north of Cape Coral, but south of Tampa. Hurricanes lose steam once they hit land.

Hurricane insurance will cost you on average less than $500 per year for full cost replacement of your home in the event of severe damage. I discuss Insurance in depth on page 41 (Insurance):

- Hazard (Fire, Theft, Lightning) – see http://www.stateofflorida.com/Portal/DesktopDefault.aspx?tabid=20
- Flood Insurance (FEMA - Federal Emergency Management Agency) http://www.fema.gov/plan/prevent/floodplain/nfipkeywords/flood_zones.shtm
- Hurricane Insurance (usually added onto your Home Owner Insurance Policy with 2% deductible)

8.   Backup Retirement Plan

Congratulations to those of you with the ability to save for retirement and put money into an RRSP (Registered Retirement Savings Plan). According to Canadian statistics most people don't contribute to an RRSP or save very little for their retirement years.

http://www.theglobeandmail.com/globe-investor/personal-finance/rrsp-contributions-to-keep-dropping/article1427396/

The reasons for this are unclear but life itself tends to be very expensive. Although RRSPs are tax shelters, they only form part of available funds at retirement. Other sources of income may exist such as:

- possible inheritance
- possible company pension / government pension / old age security
- selling of your home, cottage, boats, cars
- equity in your home
- sources of fixed income (Bonds, GICs, Dividends)
- setting up a home office or consulting business
- leveraging a passion or hobby to generate extra income (i.e. open a Bed & Breakfast, Artist)

Life expectancies for both men and women have increased over the years (http://www.cbc.ca/canada/story/2008/01/14/death-stats.html).

Most may end up trimming their lifestyles to accommodate the available funds, versus the other way around. Think about that for a minute. How many of us know exactly what we want to do in retirement, then estimate the future costs of those activities and start a plan to meet those financial targets? Very few of us have the time, patience, knowledge about what we want to be doing, or fortitude to embark on such a planning exercise. Visit any book store and you'll see many books in the Finance and Personal Wealth sections devoted to this very topic.

For those that do have RRSPs, how have they performed over the years? Are they meeting your financial targets? Statistics show that if you invested in stocks in 1999, your net worth would have been relatively flat over the last 10 years. More and more stock trades are being done by computers and hedge fund managers that create volatility like the "Flash Crash" experienced in May 2010 when the Dow Jones dropped an astounding 600 points in 5 minutes (http://en.wikipedia.org/wiki/Flash_crash) only to recover. Depending on the stock market for your financial independence as your only vehicle has proven to be risky.

Investing in real estate is just another investment class, helping you with diversification. However, investing in Florida will help you diversify some investments into a foreign real estate market, just in case the Canadian Real estate market falters or stalls. After all, British Columbia has recently shown that it is ranked as one of the top 10 most expensive places for real estate in North America, behind California.

Investing in Florida will also provide you with currency diversification. When the USD gains strength against world currencies, having an asset valued in US Dollars will provide an additional premium to you once you sell your asset and convert it to Canadian or perhaps into EUROs if you decide you'd like to buy a place in Tuscany or South of France.

Investing in Real Estate is mostly a passive investment. It doesn't require a lot of effort on your part other that keeping it maintained and in good working order. You actually get to keep your day job and generate income while these investments work for you. The real benefit that I see for Florida Real Estate investing is the income you can generate with Vacation Rentals. There are several well-known websites like http://www.vacationrentals.com and http://www.vrbo.com that allow vacationing families and couples to rent a property for most times less than what Hotels and Resorts will charge per night.

The reason why many vacationers choose vacation rentals is because they know they can get a private pool, a full kitchen with all amenities, usually 3 bedrooms with 2+ bathrooms that can accommodate 6-8 people. It's basically better value for the dollar. The average home rental per month in Florida is around $3,000 USD per month depending on views and amenities. If you wanted to rent the property on an annual rental you would normally get about $1,000 / month. Therefore, renting it as a vacation rental means you can make your annual earnings in one third of the time.

You can also use it yourself or continue renting it on a weekly basis for families wanting a summer escape to the beach when kids are off during the summer. You get the idea.

Owning a vacation rental can be a money machine. It can fund the things you most like to do at retirement. One of those retirement things could be going down to Florida to use that money to golf, swim or snorkel at the beach, go boating, marlin fishing, shop at the outlets, eat at great seafood restaurants, see dolphins swimming near the shores. Did I mention you wouldn't have to pay for any Hotel?

Rental Type	Rental Period	Rent/Month	Rent Collected During Period	Extra Income (off peak season)
Annual	Jan-Dec (12 months)	$1,000	$12,000	N/A
Vacation	Dec-Mar (4 months)	$3,000	$12,000	$2,000/month or $800/week

9. An investment you can improve

Florida real estate values right now are low due to the over speculation of investors climbing into the market between 2004 and 2008. It was certainly a gold rush of sorts. To give you an idea of what sort of frenzy that went on, I'll share this story with you. As I went down to Florida in 2008 for an investment home shopping trip, I saw a bright yellow sign with black marker writing that said "Must Sell Home Fast - Turn Here" at the side of the road. I decided to turn and see what the rush was all about. I spoke to the owner of this 3,000 square foot home with 5 bedrooms overlooking a beautiful lake. Although the house was gorgeous and a real steal for $180,000 I was more captivated by his story.

He was a CFO for a very large American corporation and told me how he started investing in homes about 5 years ago. He had accumulated over 25 homes that he rented. His next step was a down payment to a gated community development where he was going to buy a lot of 50 homes. Right then was when bottom fell out of the market in 2008. He was now struggling to unload properties at a major discount to avoid going into bankruptcy which would impact his ability to act as a CFO.

Since there was such a building boom that went on, you will basically see two categories of homes. Those that have been there since the early 1960s with amazing locations and views on waterways that can take a sailboat out to the Gulf of Mexico in minutes, to newer larger homes that have vaulted ceilings, lots of pot lighting, granite counter tops and newer Manibloc plumbing systems.

The choice is yours, and I own both types, but I can tell you that upgrading an older home with an amazing location will appreciate more over time. Two of my homes are Gulf access homes. The one that I paid $220,000 for sold for $655,000 in 2005. Will it go back to $655,000? Probably not anytime soon, but my investment horizon is long. If I do plan to sell, it may be 15-20 years from now but why would I? I can make an income with it as a vacation rental during my retirement years. Below are some before and after pictures of the kitchen and pool deck on a 100ft wide Canal. Your view beyond the pool is of your neighbors Yachts on their boat lifts. By the way, dolphins, manatees and stingrays come to swim in these canals.

What about fixing up your property? In my experience, the labour rates are very fair and I found them cheap compared to quotes you would get from trades in cities like Toronto. They also give you a quote without taxes so you can get a lot of work done for the money. Not to mention that the construction trades are really hungry for work.

These pictures below are from an outdated kitchen for a house I purchased in 2009 and hired someone to buy and install new cabinets for $6,000 and convert to countertops to granite for another $3,000.They also removed the bulkheads in the ceiling and installed pot lights instead. New appliances of course cost another $3,000. The floor was laminate wood flooring and was replaced with porcelain tile installed on the diagonal throughout the entire house for $4,000 labour and $4,000 for the 20" porcelain tiles. I also had the entire house re-plumbed from copper to CPVC for $3,000. Try and get your house re-plumbed for that amount with taxes, product and labour included.

10. An investment that is understood

Warren Buffet, the great investor always said, "Invest in things you understand" http://sites.google.com/site/willyakibusinessschool/warren-buffett-series-1/buffett-story---gave-37billion-to-bill-gates-foundation/warren-buffett-talk-at-mba.

The latest stock market meltdown involved products like ABS, CDO, CDS products with little transparency to the underlying derivative products that even large institutional investment firms didn't understand.
http://en.wikipedia.org/wiki/Asset-backed_security
http://en.wikipedia.org/wiki/Collateralized_debt_obligation
http://en.wikipedia.org/wiki/Credit_default_swap

Warren also said, "Only buy something that you'd be perfectly happy to hold if the market shut down for 10 years"

http://www.brainyquote.com/quotes/authors/w/warren_buffett_2.html.

A real estate investment certainly falls into this category and is highly regulated.

Real Estate should be part of a diversified portfolio of investments (Blue Chip stocks producing growth and dividends, Treasury, Government and Municipal Bonds, metals like Gold and Silver and Real Estate).

Remember that this type of real estate is a specific type of investment; it is an Income Property. A cottage North of Toronto is not an investment but something you enjoy, unless you rent it out. You want the investment to produce dividends. If you had to borrow to own it, you want tenants in it to help you pay off that debt.

With 4 properties in Florida and a home in Toronto to live in myself, I have 5 families working to pay off my investments. It's like running a small company with employees, except they pay me, versus the other way around, and in turn I pay my creditors (the banks). Now that's using leverage in a smart way to produce wealth over time, slowly but assuredly.

Let me repeat something I said, "It's like running a small company with employees". How many people can do that and still have a day job with a salary. That's maximum revenue while managing expenses. Read any of Robert Kiyosaki's books on Rich Dad, Poor Dad which basically says that the person who runs a Business is in the richest quadrant of his 4 quadrant mapping. The reason is simple; you can help from the government with tax breaks.

http://www.richdad.com/default.aspx

Where to invest in Florida

Different areas of Florida were affected during the Mortgage Meltdown. For example, Key West didn't fall in price as much as areas like Miami, Cape Coral, or even Tampa, where much investment speculation was going on by investors. For a great resource on cities you would be interested in investing in, please check out the link below to run your comparison between cities.

http://www.city-data.com/city/Florida.html

The first decision I had to make was do I want to be North in Pensacola/Destin Beach Resorts (shown on the right) a very popular vacation destination or did I want venture more towards Central Florida in Tampa/Orlando/Daytona Beach or South in Naples/Miami/Key West. Coast to coast distance is typically 2-3 hours' drive apart.

I assessed environmental factors like temperature/hurricane/flood exposure differences (http://ff.org/centers/csspp/pdf/20070709_florida.pdf) between North and South but there wasn't much variance. I analyzed access by International Airports and then also looked at what Tourists like to do; keeping in mind this would be a vacation rental one day.

Although North Pensacola/Destin has some of the world's whitest beaches, so does Siesta Keys near Tampa/Sarasota (http://www.findsouthwestfloridahomes.com/sarasota-real-estate.php) in Central and so does Fort Myers/Sanibel Island (http://www.findsouthwestfloridahomes.com/sanibel-island-real-estate.php) in South West and so does Miami/Key West in South East.

Since Key West still had expensive real estate but was still accessible by car from Miami (3 hours' drive) or by Ferry Shuttle (http://www.keywesttours.us/?event=offer.detail&offerId=5864) one way from Fort Myers beach (3 hours) I decided that although very beautiful, it was too specific a destination to own there but could be accessed easily should the need arise.

That left me with either Central (Tampa/Orlando) or South West (Fort Myers Beach, Bonita Springs, Estero, Naples):

http://www.findsouthwestfloridahomes.com/fort-myers-beach-real-estate.php
http://www.findsouthwestfloridahomes.com/bonita-springs-real-estate.php
http://www.findsouthwestfloridahomes.com/estero-real-estate.php
http://www.findsouthwestfloridahomes.com/naples-real-estate.php

or South East (Miami, Fort Lauderdale).When comparing prices, I noticed that prices were still higher in Naples and Tampa. Naples has a well-established community and did not have as much speculative buying. The city architecture was inspired by and built to the same style as the city in Italy itself. This city is host to some of the world's most expensive real estate with many coastal homes going for $5 Million plus. This city was out of my investment league. However as I ventured slightly north by 10 minute drive I found Bonita Springs, Estero, Fort Myers Beach then Cape Coral. This South-West area was also 90 minute drive to Miami, across Interstate Highway 75, also known as Alligator Alley because you drive through the Everglades National Park.

Bonita Springs has a unique "Old Florida Lifestyle" feel whereas Estero has an upwardly mobile younger feel to it with countless Gated Communities cropping up everywhere and Coconut Point Mall as the shopping and dining Mecca located in the centre. Although Bonita Springs is along the Gulf coast, Estero is more inland, but still only 30 minute drive to either Fort Myers Beach or Bonita Beach. During winter (peak season) that drive could increase to 1 hour as the roads become congested with the influx of seasonal renters and vacationers, something to keep in mind. If a Gated Community captures your interest then Estero has many to choose from, however, your costs can be high as I explain in the next section.

Fort Myers beach is very similar to other beach towns like Myrtle Beach, Virginia Beach, Daytona Beach and Miami Beach. It can become very noisy with bikers and young people partying to all hours. It is a great place to own a rental property because you can get really high weekly rents since this is a destination spot that people return to year after year, especially during March break when it's even hard to find vacancies. However, because of the type of tenants you will get, the probability of damage is higher because people do let loose when they stay for that period and live care free for that week. Besides, most small 2 bedroom homes go for $400,000 and up, many built on stilts. The county restriction forbids building on the lower level (usually where the cars are parked) where you could add 2 more bedrooms. They are considered illegal or against building code.

Then there's Fort Myers. This town is changing quickly. It used to have an old feel to it and felt like your Mother and Father's retirement town when Mobile Homes and Trailer Parks were common vacation or retirement residences. Most of those are now gone and the Harbour Side is developing quickly with many High-Rise Condo Residences.

Ft. Myers is a working town and many people come from different areas like Lehigh Acres, North Fort Myers or Cape Coral to work at the various businesses Universities (Keiser, Hodges , Edison and nearby FGCU) or large Hospitals (Gulf Coast Medical Center, VA Hospital). Why is this important? Having tenants that work at Hospitals, Police, Fireman or Universities as staff offers lower threats of job loss or relocations, resulting in steady rent and better tenants. A drive to Ft. Myers beach and Sanibel Island is only 20-40 minutes depending on season.

The Median house price Ft. Myers area peaked in late 2005 at $322,300. Three years later, it had plummeted to $106,900. A reliance on construction jobs no longer available pushed the unemployment rate in the area of Lehigh Acres and Fort Myers to 14% by the summer of 2009. Property values in Lehigh Acres dropped 25% in 2008, and another 50% in 2009. (http://en.wikipedia.org/wiki/Lehigh_Acres,_Florida).

Just North of Ft. Myers is the Caloosahatchee River (http://en.wikipedia.org/wiki/Caloosahatchee_River) with 3 bridges to Cape Coral and North Ft. Myers. Cape Coral (http://en.wikipedia.org/wiki/Cape_Coral,_Florida) also referred to as "The Cape" by its locals, is known for its salt water canals with access to the Gulf of Mexico. With over 400 miles (640 km) of navigable waterways, Cape Coral has more miles of canals than any other city on earth, including Venice, Italy.

Cape Coral is the most populous city between Tampa and Miami. As of April 2009, Cape Coral was the 9th largest city in Florida by population and the 3rd largest geographically. More than 60 percent of the population is between the ages of 15-64 and residents under 25 outnumber residents over 65. Southwest Florida's 18-24 age groups are growing at a faster rate than the state of Florida and the United States.

Like many communities in Florida, Cape Coral experienced a real estate boom during the 2000s and was hit hard by the following real estate bust beginning in 2006. As of April 23, 2009 the area is listed number 3 out of 25 for the highest Foreclosure Cities in the US according to RealtyTrac. Foreclosures in this market quickly adjusted property values back down to a level that the city had not seen in many years. In late 2009, a new home could be purchased for under $80,000.

I decided to purchase real estate in Cape Coral because of the Navigable Waterways out to the Gulf, close access to Ft. Myers for working population, close access to beaches Ft. Myers Beach and Sanibel, golf courses and Yacht clubs and close access to all amenities like airport (RSW), shopping, dining, entertainment, but most of all price and the high Foreclosure rate. Orlando and Miami would have also been good choices which also had large price drops and Foreclosures but Cape Coral lies directly in between those two cities and provides Water front properties with Sailboat access to the Gulf of Mexico that you cannot get in Miami or Tampa for the same price. Orlando of course is inland. Did I mention that Cape Coral has over 400 miles of waterway canals, more than Venice Italy? If you love boating, yachting or sailing, this place is for you. That's basically how I narrowed down my choices after visiting all of these cities.

What to invest in Florida

There are basically the following types of real estate investments available:

- Condos
- Townhomes or Villas
- Single Family Homes
- Multi-Family Homes
- Land

Condos

Condos come in Low-rise (1-3 floors) Mid-Rise (3-7 floors) and High rise (8+ floors) variations. Condos are good investments if you plan to own a place as your vacation spot and want to use it for that purpose. Over time, it *might* appreciate in value and you *could* be selling for a profit. It provides the convenience of arriving with just a small suitcase, using it and locking it up when you are done. The building and the grounds are maintained for you as part of your monthly HOA (Home Owners Association) fee, also referred to as Condo Fee and building insurance costs as usually included as part of those costs.

You gain convenience but you give up autonomy. You are part owner of a building and you are limited by the rules of the Condominium and HOA deed restrictions. The deed restrictions can vary widely, from types of vehicles you are allowed to park in the outside parking spaces and garage, to pets you are allowed to own, to colours you want to paint your Condo or who is allowed to rent your condo and how often. You have voting privileges as part owner but you need to be present at the meetings and become active in the Condo Association in order to effectively argue for change. This may not be practical if you are only there for vacations and renting it out to your friends and family.

You need to be careful when looking at Condos. Before investing you need to look at the balance sheets for cash reserves. This will show you how good a job a Condo Association has been doing with the money it collects in HOA fees from the tenants. This cash is needed for unexpected expenses like fixing Elevators or paving roof tops or fixing broken Air Conditioners. It is run like a corporation with an elected board of directors who typically hire property managers to manage the condo. Also find out how many units are vacant in the building. With the number of Foreclosures going on, less Condo owners means less HOA fees coming in.

This will drain the cash reserves very quickly as expenses continue but income drops. Also talk to people in the building that live there to find out how quickly things get fixed. I did this when I looked at Miami Condos and you'll quickly get the opposite side of what the Real Estate agent or Condo owners will tell you. You need to form a median opinion between those viewpoints as to what the truth is about the Condo.

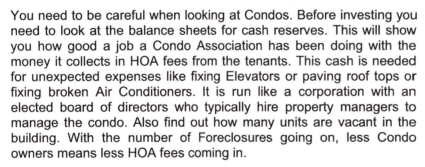

You need to understand what the Condo fees are. Have they been increased or decreased over the years. If you are looking at renting this Condo out to make income, read the Condo Association by-laws and documents and ask how many times you can rent out your condo annually. The most generous policy I found was 12 times per year for a minimum 1 month duration stay. How many people can afford to get away for 4 weeks?

In my investment search, I have researched Condos and saw many of them. In my opinion, I don't consider them as great investments for generating income; my primary investment goal. The main reasons are:

- Too many limitations and restrictions for renting out to whomever I wanted (i.e. rent out monthly or weekly)
- Lack of control on Expenses (i.e. HOA fees going up over time, other tenants foreclosing)
- Limited ability to improve property for greater re-sale value (i.e. deed restrictions)
- Limited ability to vote for proper representation (i.e. remote ownership)
- Newer Condos going up near yours with better amenities (possibly obstructing views and affecting re-sale value)

There are some Condos, especially in Miami and Aventura that will allow you to rent them out weekly or even daily. These are really Hotel Condo conversions. They were hotels at one time but have sold the units to investors. They will be typically under 500 square feet, no kitchen, one bathroom, 2 double beds and a dresser (think of a typical Holiday Inn type room). However, you will get a balcony that could overlook the Ocean. These Condo Hotels will most often come with reservation desks that can check in your guests and provide them with the keys to your condo. Some reservation desks take up to 50% of your rental income but they provide a service to fill your room with potential vacationers through their own websites. Some may offer daily Maid service for a fee.

In the end, you really need to work out the numbers to see if it makes financial sense for you to make profits. Create a spreadsheet like I did below to give you a financial analytic view to whether the property will generate profits or carry itself.

I list the property with its price, address, MLS #, square footage, beds, baths, and parking spaces for my real estate agent to lookup. I add up the monthly HOA fees, annual property taxes plus my monthly mortgage interest to give me an annual cost. I then put in what I can get for rental income.

Look at the 1st entry which is actually a Condo Hotel. The light green shaded area shows you the figures. Add in the Property Management fee and your occupancy rate. Notice how small the unit is; 310 square feet, 0 bedrooms, 1 Bath, 1 Parking space. In order to make a profit you need to rent this unit out 5 months of the year (November-March). The largest inhibitors preventing you from making profits is mainly the high HOA fee ($622) and the high management fee (50%). This does not look like a good investment as you are losing $2,386 every year.

The 2nd entry is a 654 sq ft 1 bed / 1 bath / 1 parking spot Condo on Ocean Drive in South Miami Beach (SOBE). The brown shaded area assumes renting it as an Annual Rental and getting Monthly income. This is a better investment as it can produce a profit of $2,843 every year. This profit can help towards your down payment for this investment or to absorb Tax and HOA fee increases.

Price	Address	MLS	SF	Bd	Ba	Pk	Unit #	HOA	Taxes	Interest	HOA+ TAX+ INT	Annual Rental (Month)	P/L (Annual)	Weekly Rental (Week)	Mgmt Fee	% Occ	Annual Income (Weekly)	P/L (Weekly)
$149,000	1801 Collins Av	M1356396	310	0	1	1	1205	$622	$2,652	-$590	$10,706			$800	50%	40%	$8,320	-$2,386
$159,000	325 Ocean Dr	F1026746	654	1	1	1		$294	$3,800	-$629	$7,957	$900	$2,843					

Web Tools I used for Miami condo hunting were:
http://miamiinvest.com/
http://www.naplesgulfliving.com/site/index.php
http://www.miamicondolifestyle.com/english/miami-condos.php
http://www.sunnyislesmiamirealestate.com/Miami_Condos_For_Sale.htm

Townhomes

Townhouses may also be called twin Villas depending on where you look. A common trait for Townhomes is that they share a common wall, floor/ceiling with other units. They can be side by side or on top of each other.

Townhouses tend to come in at a lower price point than Single Family Homes because they save the builder some materials and some land costs that would normally go between the homes. Townhouses or twin Villas that are side by side may provide individual pools for each home. The ones on top of each other usually provide a common community pool. If you are in a Gated Community, you usually have access to a recreation or club house. The really upscale ones can provide boutique shops, games room and movie theatre.

Should you invest in a Gated Community? From a pure investment standpoint if you plan to get maximum income over expense, probably not. The HOA fees are high because you are getting all the amenities of a country club atmosphere to enjoy for those fees. Are tenants willing to pay extra rent for an exercise room, an 8,000 square foot community pool, waterfalls along the drive into their neighborhood, 24 hour security? Chances are most tenants will not want to cover those costs 100% for you. However, if your goal is to occupy this investment yourself one day, then maybe it's worth it to cover the shortfall in rent to mark your place in the sun one day. So this can become more of a

personal choice than strictly financial. My decision after looking at this extensively was to make my money between now and retirement and then with the rental income I can generate from my vacation rentals, put that money into the gated community I want to be in at that time. Builders keep building them and they keep getting more grandiose. Tenants need the basics and will not pay you for luxurious amenities.

The challenge with Gated Communities is the same as with Condos. You need to understand the community policy on how often you can rent out your property and to whom and what is the approval process? Your HOA fee will usually include, trash collection, irrigation, security, street lighting, lawn mowing and shrub and bush trimming. It is not that uncommon that when renting your unit to guests, they may need to be interviewed first by the Association before being accepted. They want to see who is coming into the community as their job is to protect the community atmosphere.

With Gated Community home purchases you will most often be saddled with also paying a CDD fee (Community Development Deposit) fee (http://www.ccfj.net/CDDhiddencostliving.html).

A CDD fee is the shared amount of debt that needs to be paid off by all Community members for the development of the surrounding landscapes, waterfalls, Gate Houses at the entrance that were built before all the homes were built. As Florida's population boomed, CDDs were created to shift the burden of building roads and utility lines away from cash-starved municipal and county governments. The massive costs of building the infrastructure are financed by the developer with a key CDD incentive: tax-free municipal bonds. The bonds pay for not only roads and utilities, but also amenities such as clubhouses, pools, tennis courts and golf courses that entice middle-class buyers yearning for a loftier lifestyle. Rather than paying everything up front, homeowners pay the ultimate costs for the amenities over a span of 15 to 30 years.

As with Condos, you need to crunch the numbers and see how much costs go into HOA, CDD, Taxes and other expenses like Pool care, if you have a private pool. Then determine your best scenario for rental income. Most

Gated Communities that I visited like Bella Terra (http://www.findsouthwestfloridahomes.com/bella-terra-real-estate.php) in Estero Florida will allow you to rent it out for 3 months twice a year. If you know of some snow birds that could stay the whole season, then this will help you offset the annual costs of such an investment.

The amenities of a Gated Community like central Club House with restaurants for dining, games rooms, large swimming pool, exercise rooms and regular social events are the best-selling features for a Gated Community. This helps draw potential renters, particularly those that are retired or semi-retired and can afford to stay for 3-4 months. The costs are higher for you but it may allow you to use it yourself in the spring or summer months to enjoy with friends and family.

The grounds will be kept appealing as many have deed restrictions (like no RVs allowed in your driveway). This can be a comfort knowing that potential buyers coming to see your home won't be distracted by neighborhood decay.

Single Family Homes

Single Family Homes offer the largest type of selection, location, and flexibility of investment options. You might find something with Water views or sail boat access or you might find a home with a Golf Course in your backyard. Either way, the selection is enormous, all you need to do is basically make your list of requirements, plug in your criteria, enter your price range and search away.

I would recommend looking for homes with in-ground pools as Florida has the climate that almost demands it during the summer months and if you want to rent it out as a vacation rental during the winter peak season, you should also look at having a pool heater.

A solar pool heater can cost anywhere from $3,000-$5,000, installed. Although a solar pool heater is cost efficient, it does not warm water effectively if the outside temperature goes near freezing like the winter of 2009. An electric pool heater could however get the water warmer but your electricity bills would obviously feel the effects of that. However, with vacation rentals that have pool heaters, the renters are usually responsible for the electricity bills during their stay. A meter reading is done before and after their rental period and deducted from their deposit. If you do happen to find an incredible deal without a pool, you can have one installed for as little as $30,000 (includes pool cage). You'll obviously get better rental income with a pool.

A barrel tile roof is not a must but it will save you roof repairs or replacement costs over the years, and this is usually a large investment. The heat can be intense during the summer but a barrel tile roof absorbs and insulates your house from the solar heat. They tend to last about 75 years.

Watch out for Chinese Drywall. The housing boom between the years 2004 and 2007 actually encountered a shortage of drywall to finish the inside of the homes being built. Drywall was then imported from China to fulfill the demand. Unfortunately, the quality of drywall coming from China had too much sulfur mixture in it. Air conditioners failed every two months; electrical outlets corroded to black powder; residents suffered constant nosebleeds and persistent coughs. Insurance companies won't cover the claim citing their policies don't cover this type of damage and blame the builders. The only solution is to rip it all out and re-drywall the house. You will know that a house has Chinese drywall in it if it smells like rotten eggs, but it's not always easily detectable. Get a home inspection done to ensure you don't encounter this situation.

Most contracts in South Florida today, especially Foreclosures, are AS-IS FARBAR contracts. A FARBAR contract is a contract that has been approved by both the Florida Association of Realtors (FAR) and the Florida Bar Association (BAR).
http://www.trulia.com/voices/Home_Buying/What_is_a_As_Is_FarBAr_contract_Thanks-126616

Once you sign this contract, it puts the ownership on your side to have the home inspected to ensure there's no Chinese Drywall or other damage and prevents you from suing for damages after both parties agree to the sale (sold AS-IS). Also take special note in what year the home was built and have your home inspection done and you should be fine.

Many homes in Florida were on a septic system instead of central city water and sewer. Septic systems involve a well about 10-12 feet under the ground and takes in salt water seeping in from the water table. Much of the plumbing was in copper since the early 1960s and many homes had water heater tanks with copper containers. Once the city started converting homes over to city water, the water was distributed to the homes with pressure to push it to all the homes when you turn on the tap. Problems were discovered as Water Heater Tanks started bursting and leaking. The problem was that the salt in the septic water was corroding the inside of the Water Heater tanks. Once pressure was applied inside the plumbing system, the tanks with weak and corroded areas burst open and sprung a leak. Most Water Heaters in Florida are in the garages and it was said that you could see water coming from many peoples garages down the driveway towards the street.

Today, most homes in Florida are no longer in copper but in CPVC, a plastic type of pipe. It is highly durable and non-corroding. If buying an older house, make sure you have CPVC plumbing throughout. If the home is newer, it may even have a ManiBloc plumbing system installed.

Air Conditioners are used almost 8 months out of the year in Florida homes. It is not just important for comfortable living; Air Conditioners are used to take moisture out of the air, resulting in less humidity. With less humidity, there's less opportunity for Black Mold to grow (shown on the right). Black mold contains spores like mushrooms and if inhaled can cause sickness and severe headaches. According to the CDC (Center of Disease Control) black mold is responsible for over "100 cases of lung disorders".

Another home feature you should have on your list of criteria is an Irrigation system with automatic sprinkler system. Most homes have this, but not all. Without it, your lawn will look dry and brown very quickly and become susceptible to broadleaf weeds and insects. If your home doesn't have it, it will cost you about $1500-$2000 on average to install. Not a huge expense in the entire scheme of things but one less expense if it's included.

Single family homes provide you with the ability to increase their value over time with upgrades. Why upgrade a property when you are only going to rent it? The main reason for upgrading and improving your property is for reducing your capital gains tax and to give your property market appeal so that it sells quickly on the market when you decide to sell. Property upgrades can be as simple as planting Royal Palm trees on your property to give it curb appeal and a Florida look. In 2008 I was able to get 20 feet high Royal Palms installed for $200. It used to cost $1,000 each prior to 2005.

Consider these two property scenarios:

Property A:	SCENARIO 1	SCENARIO 2
Purchase Price for home:	$200,000	$200,000
Capital Improvements to home:	$0	$0
Sale Price obtained for home:	$300,000	$300,000
Capital Gain	$100,000	$100,000
Taxable Amount (50% of capital gain)	$50,000	$50,000
Taxed at current Marginal Tax Rate (37%)	$18,500	$18,500
Property B:		
Purchase Price for home:	$200,000	$200,000
Capital Improvements to home:	$ 70,000	$ 70,000
Sale Price obtained for home:	$300,000	$370,000
Capital Gain	$ 30,000	$100,000
Taxable amount (50% of capital gain)	$15,000	$ 50,000
Taxed at current Marginal Tax Rate (37%)	$5,550	$ 18,500

Let's first look at SCENARIO 1 between two Properties. Taxes owed on the Capital Gain for Property B ($5,500) are lower than for Property A ($18,500) because we claimed "Capital Improvements" made on Property B each year on our tax submissions.

You have two choices when it comes to filing for Taxes on Capital Improvements. You can file every year and claim those costs as expenses against your income (i.e. Personal Income, Rental Income) or you can claim them as Capital Improvements to your property to be added up and deducted from the Capital Gain when you sell. Capital Gain is the difference between purchase price and selling price assuming prices go up. If they go down, it becomes a Capital Loss which can be used to offset gains made elsewhere in your portfolio, like stocks, bonds and other real estate.

Which do you choose? That is really a Tax-me-now or Tax-me-later question and will depend on your situation, like age, income, current and future financial goals.

If personal income is currently very high for you and you want tax relief and you plan to sell this property yourself during your lifetime when you will not be making any income other than pension then perhaps you may elect to claim your capital improvements within the current tax years.

However, when you go to sell, you'll pay on the net gain, which may not matter much to you if you are mainly interested in getting the tax relief today. However, what if your property doubles in value in the time you want to sell it? Is that really possible?

Consider that most properties sold for double or almost triple what they were listed for in 2005. If you plan on holding it for a long time (20+ years) then your chances are good. The table on the right shows a 2% increase in real estate values every year, on average. After 22 years, your property bought at $200,000 has increased by 55% over that period. That's a conservative estimate if the purchase price was considered fair market value to begin with. However, remember, the fair market values for most properties have been slashed by 50% or more in the recent years.

Consider this quote from TrimTabs Investment Research on January 27, 2011:

"It's taken three years to process $1 trillion in foreclosed homes. At that rate, it will take more than five years for the amount of each individual's mortgage debt, relative to their income, to get back to levels that were the norm in this country before the housing bubble, according to a report from TrimTabs Investment Research.

That basically says by year 2016 we'll recover most of the correction that has started in the housing market in 2007 – a 9 year recovery, not 22 years.

Look at the expense column for each year. Could you spend that much on the property every year? I'm sure you could if you really tried, but expenses like $8,000 would buy you a lot. I re-plumbed my

Year	Expense	Market Price
2008	$ 8,000.00	$ 200,000.00
2009	$ 3,000.00	$ 204,000.00
2010	$ 2,000.00	$ 208,080.00
2011	$ 1,500.00	$ 212,241.60
2012	$ 1,800.00	$ 216,486.43
2013	$ 400.00	$ 220,816.16
2014	$ 800.00	$ 225,232.48
2015	$ 25.00	$ 229,737.13
2016	$ 999.00	$ 234,331.88
2017	$ 1,234.00	$ 239,018.51
2018	$ 8,700.00	$ 243,798.88
2019	$ 1,200.00	$ 248,674.86
2020	$ 2,300.00	$ 253,648.36
2021	$ 155.00	$ 258,721.33
2022	$ 2,300.00	$ 263,895.75
2023	$ 822.00	$ 269,173.67
2024	$ 233.00	$ 274,557.14
2025	$ 542.00	$ 280,048.28
2026	$ 276.00	$ 285,649.25
2027	$ 123.00	$ 291,362.23
2028	$ 2,234.00	$ 297,189.48
2029	$ 123.00	$ 303,133.27
2030	$ 77.00	$ 309,195.93
	$ 38,843.00	$ 309,195.93

Capital Gain:	$ 109,195.93
Years Held:	22
Less Capital Improvements	$ 38,843.00
Net Capital Gain	$ 70,352.93
Tax 50% of Gain	$ 35,176.47
Marginal Tax Rate	37%
Taxes Owed	$ 13,015.29

entire home in Florida from Copper to CPVC for $3,000. A brand new Air Conditioner will cost you about $3,000 and a Pool Heater will cost you about $3,000.

My point here is that you'd be hard pressed to spend that kind of money to offset your gains in personal and rental income. Remember that you'll have other ongoing maintenance expenses that will offset your rental income, like Lawn Cutting services, Lawn Fertilization and Pool Care.

My choice was to claim the Capital Improvements over time and have them deducted from the capital gain I make when selling the home. Remember that one house I purchased for $220,000 once sold for $655,000 in 2005. If I'm making a $435,000 Capital Gain, I want to keep as much of it as possible as my retirement cushion. It doesn't make it a better choice, just a personal one. Choose what's right for your situation with help from your Tax accountant.

Your next personal choice might be how many homes should you buy and at what price point? Should you buy $1 million home overlooking the Ocean now for sales at $450,000, or buy a home at $150,000 in a good area or should you by 3 homes for $50,000 each.

In real estate, agents will always tell you to buy based on location, location, location. I can tell you that a $50,000 home will not be located in premiere locations. They are cheap, and with a little tender loving care, can be cleaned up and rented out. Your chances for a positive cash flow situation are best for these types of homes. However, they will demand more of your time when purchasing to go down and clean them up (they are $50,000 for a reason). They usually attract lower end tenants that may not always have stable jobs and you'll find yourself finding new tenants every year. You'll spend your time dealing with tenants that have issues like, job loss, job relocations (construction trades) or even domestic problems like separation, divorce etc. You may have rent collection issues. My personal opinion is that this will become more of a headache for you to manage in the long run than what it's worth. What is it worth anyway? You'll get positive cash flow but what can you sell your property at in 10 years from now?

What about the $1 Million property for $450,000 with ocean view? You will find it hard to get positive cash flow for a property like this. If you are buying something like this, then it's really a property for you and you are looking at it as a consumer instead of an investor. That's ok, if that's your goal, to be in it sometime soon.

My choice was to go down the middle and shoot for the best locations with the most fallen prices for homes you can fix up but have amazing views or something unique that you cannot buy at a Home Depot like Sailboat access to the Gulf. There are only so many properties out there with that kind of feature.

Multi-Family Homes

This category of home is somewhat similar to Twin-Villas up to a multi-tenanted building complex where 2, 4 or 6 families can live. The costs for a 2 family complex are about equal to single family home in terms of price but you can get 2 families in where you collect rent. Think of a 2000 square foot home with 4 bedrooms and 2 bathrooms, and then split it into two with a wall separating each unit. That will give you two 1000 square foot units with 2 bedrooms and 1 bathroom each.

You won't get as much rent for each unit as you would for a single family home, but combined, your chances are better for exceeding your rental income over a single family home.

You need to ask yourself what your goals are. If you want a place to stay while in Florida but generate some income at the same time, then this might make sense as you could rent one unit and use the other for yourself. If your goal is strictly for positive cash flow and have steady rental income and not worry about resale value in the future, then this might also make sense. However, remember that when you want to sell these units, you are selling them together to another like-minded investor with the same goals as you had when you first bought it. It doesn't attract the same market as buyers looking for a single family home. You are looking for a specific buyer and by doing this you are limiting your market exposure. For this reason alone, I'm not in favour of such investments.

Land

If buying a single family home is like buying a stock that can appreciate in value over time and produces dividends (rental income) then buying land is like buying gold. It doesn't generate any income but it could gain in value over time. It may also cost you less and require less maintenance or ongoing costs. Some plots of land can be purchased for as little as $7,000 or for lots with access to open water, $150,000 and up.

If your intent is to hold a lot where you plan to build a home on it then this might make sense. After you build the home, if your location is excellent (sailboat access, no bridges to open water) and you did well with getting a home build, in a good market you could potentially sell for a profit. Otherwise, it's really not an investment until you put a house or building on it. For that reason, I would not invest in it as my dollars are not working for me right away. With a house, my dollars can start working immediately and one day I could tear down the house and build a new one.

By the way, did you know that there's a small loophole in Southwest Florida municipal code that says that if you tear down your entire house and leave just one wall up, then it is considered a renovation, not a new home build? Why is that important? If you tear down everything, then your property is subject to new tax assessments and impact fees. This may not be in place forever but I did see many lots with just one wall standing and learned this was common practice.

When is the best time to buy in Florida

This article was published on November 1, 2010, just before the Mid-term US elections.

U.S. home prices expected to slide another 8%

Les Christie, staff writer, On Monday November 1, 2010, 6:54 am EDT

The robo-signing controversy is just another issue that the already sluggish housing market didn't need -- but most analysts do not think it will have far-reaching impact. Nevertheless, the housing market still faces many problems: a weak economy, sluggish hiring, tight mortgage underwriting, falling home prices, and slowing sales.
http://money.cnn.com/real_estate/foreclosure_fiasco/

Then there's the potentially disastrous number of foreclosures that may occur over the coming years. "The market faces much bigger problems than the robo-signing issue," said Mike Larson, a housing market analyst for Weiss Research. Prime among them are declines in home prices. And while cheaper homes are good for buyers, they also speak to a housing market that won't stabilize.

Fiserv, a market analytics company, has scaled back its home price projections considerably. In February, it forecast national price gains of about 4% through the end of 2011. The company's latest prediction is for a 7.1% drop in prices between June 30, 2010 and June 30, 2011. In fact, after five months of gains, prices in the 20 largest metro areas fell 0.2% in August, according to the latest S&P/Case-Shiller report.

The good news is, "There'll be no vicious, self-reinforcing spiral down," according to Mark Zandi, chief economist with Moody's Analytics. But, he added, "more home price declines are coming." He's forecasting another 8% drop in home prices through the third quarter of 2011, which will put the total peak-to-trough decline at 34%. Even after that, in 2012, he sees very little price growth. Home prices continue to fall because sales aren't taking off. Without buyers, the market can't bottom out. New home sales continue to languish around historic lows, barely exceeding an annual rate of 307,000. Existing home sales did rise to a 4.53 million annualized rate in September, up 10%

compared with a month earlier, but are still well below the boom years. Of course, nobody is buying homes when they can't find jobs. And still more people can't hang on to their homes because they're out of work.

Nearly a million homes are expected to be repossessed this year, and analysts seem to be competing to issue the most dire forecast for future foreclosure numbers. Morgan Stanley reported that about 3.1 million borrowers are seriously delinquent with many expected to lose their homes. Zandi said more than 4 million are in trouble with half of those expected to go to foreclosure. And Laurie Goodman, of Amherst Securities, estimates the number of homes in danger of foreclosure at a whopping 11 million. Real estate analyst Kyle Lundstedt of LPS Applied Analytics said serious delinquencies will continue to spike and will not return even to the current rates -- which are already at peak levels -- until late 2012 or early 2013.

"The housing market is very fragile," said Goodman. However, Zandi sees a few factors that are positive. These include: Low interest rates; FHA, Fannie Mae and Freddie Mac all lending to qualified buyers; and an improving job picture. Zandi is especially confident that the employment picture is about to brighten. Corporate profits have spiked and, historically, hiring follows profits -- with a lag of eight to 10 months. That means companies should start hiring workers very soon, Zandi said. And once Americans start returning to work, they'll find home prices are very reasonable. Housing is the most affordable it's been since the pre-boom years. During the boom, Zandi said, prices were overvalued by about 50%; today it's close to zero.

That has attracted many investors, including foreign buyers. They've been scooping up single-family-homes and condos in hard-hit markets like Florida, the Southwest and the Midwest and renting them out. "The reason they're in these markets is because they see value," said Zandi. But, he added, "If they see the robo-signing issue continue, they could begin to exit the market. If they do, there could be more price declines. That's one reason why a foreclosure moratorium could be destructive."

http://money.cnn.com/2010/10/29/news/economy/australians_real_estate/index.htm

As you can see from the report, there is plenty of time to get into this market (right up to end of 2013) and take advantage of getting in while prices are depressed. Remember, you are investing for a long time horizon (this is not a get rich quick scheme). You are also investing with the intention to create retirement income, through vacation rentals. That's the ultimate goal here as an investment that works for you. However, there are other countries like Australia who are recognizing that the timing is right, as demonstrated in this next article.

Australians swoop in on U.S. foreclosures

By Steve Hargreaves, senior writer October 29, 2010: 11:54 AM ET

MEMPHIS, Tenn. (CNNMoney.com) -- On a recent Wednesday night, my wife and I found ourselves in an otherwise empty Beale Street bar surrounded by a group of Australian men.

"You guys from here?" they asked cheerily. "You like the area? What do you do for work?"

Despite the boozy surroundings, what could have been mistaken for friendly banter was actually research. The Australians were on a real estate tour of American cities, sussing them out before pulling the trigger on the latest trend in this hard-hit sector: snapping up foreclosed homes, renovating them, and then renting them out.

od
ith.

"America represents an opportunity, and Australians have just jumped all over it," said Andrew Allen, founder of My USA Property, who was leading the tour.

Allen's firm, which has an office in Orlando, Fla., brokers deals between Australians and real estate professionals in the United States. The real estate pros who find the foreclosed homes also fix them up and then manage them as rentals. The Australians provide the capital and -- hopefully -- collect the profits.

The properties come delivered with a clear title and a building inspector's report. The firm has arranged nearly 300 deals in the last two years in 14 U.S. cities, mostly in the Southeast and Midwest.

who
to
nes.

Allen, an Australian himself, owns eight properties in the United States. He hopes to have 30 within the next five years.

"The beauty is, the U.S. economy will recover one day," he said. "You guys have hit a rough patch, but we know you'll be back with flying colors."

It's all about natural resources. It's not just the hurting American economy that makes these deals so sweet. It's largely the complex interplay of the global economy. The Australians are riding a commodity-driven export boom. China, workshop to the world, is gobbling up ever more metal and fossil fuel, much of which comes from Australia. Among Australia's top commodity exports are coal, iron ore and gold. Unemployment in Australia is just 5.1%. Home prices, which did not fall, average $500,000. Plus, the Australian dollar is at near record highs, equal in value to its U.S. counterpart.

That means Australians have lots of cash. In many cases, Allen said his investors are taking out home equity loans to buy U.S. property. That may strike many as an all-too-familiar and risky proposition, but Allen believes it's safe. He says stricter banking regulations and a rising population will keep his country immune from a housing downturn.

A closer look at the deal. The deals themselves seem solid, at least on paper. Jim Reedy, owner of the Memphis-based property management firm Reedy and Company, said a recent sale he put together for an Australian on a $68,000 house looked something like this:

How to buy a foreclosure in a robo-signing world

With a $17,000 down payment, the monthly costs for the buyer totaled about $700. That included the mortgage payment, insurance, management fee, taxes and setting aside 12% of the rent in an emergency fund to cover maintenance and vacancies. Yet the house rents for $1,100 a month. So the buyer is making $400 a month, a 28% return on his $17,000 investment. And that's not counting any appreciation the home may see, or the currency advantage if the Australian buys now and the Aussie dollar falls in the future.

"Our business is exploding," said Reedy, who buys foreclosed properties every day, literally right off the Memphis courthouse steps. He said the recent drop in foreclosures due to the **robo-signing mess** has crimped sales, but that he expects foreclosures to pick right back up again early next year. Reedy is making money on both the home sale and the management fee. He pays somewhere between $20,000 and $30,000 for the home, then hires contractors to put another $10,000 to $15,000 worth of work into it. Then he charges 8% of the monthly rent to

COURTESY TANYA MARCHIOL

manage the property, find tenants and deal with any additional repairs.

Before this year, he said most people looking to buy these homes were Americans, sometimes referred to as **vulture investors**. But now, about 30% of his clients are from overseas -- many from Australia, New Zealand and Singapore, and also some wealthy Europeans.

Nationwide phenomenon. This is happening in other parts of the country as well. In Phoenix, where real estate prices are off 50% from their peak in 2002, broker and property manager Tanya Marchiol said she has helped Australians buy 16 properties in the last six weeks. "It's crazy," she said. "They're scooping up tons of stuff." She also says she seen lots of interest from people in Canada, another place where the economy is heavily pegged to commodities. Sometimes the process involves evicting the occupants of the foreclosed homes. Some criticize this harsh reality as taking advantage of other people's misfortune. They argue it opens the market for foreclosed properties, giving banks an incentive to foreclose and not work with the homeowner.

But Allen and others in the business say it's simply the free market at work. In many cases, they say the people being foreclosed on never should have bought the place to begin with. The investors are keeping the home from falling into disrepair, and are helping put a floor under housing prices.

Not for the timid. Despite the rosy scenarios, the investments themselves are risky propositions. One financial planner strongly advised against it, unless it's just a small part of a portfolio or one can afford to buy dozens of homes. "Otherwise, it's a crap shoot," said Jon Duncan of Seneschal Advisors. "I wouldn't touch it with a ten-foot pole." But then again, the Aussies aren't exactly noted for being meek.

"Fortune favors the brave," said Max Billi, an Australian mortgage broker who just bought an Orlando condo, his first in the United States. "But I'm comfortable it's a safe bet." ∎

http://money.cnn.com/2010/10/28/real_estate/robosigner/index.htm
http://money.cnn.com/2010/08/02/real_estate/new_vulture_investing/index.htm

Can you afford to invest in Florida

Searching for and buying Real Estate is mostly an emotional exercise. It will generate a roller coaster of emotions, high and low. It preys on your desire for wealth, status, accomplishment, and for some, just for the pure "hunt" instinct or "gather" instinct for others. Emotion is a good driver that keeps you engaged but it needs to be tempered with reason and logic. If you don't have both these disciplines, it's sometimes best to partner with someone that has the opposite viewpoint as yours. In all cases, you'll need an objective tool to help you see things without emotion. I use a spreadsheet as my financial tool and will show you how to use it to your advantage for making sound financial decisions.

For my situation, I did the hunting and filtering of properties that I thought were great deals and then passed them along to my wife to review with great enthusiasm. When I was ready to almost submit an offer on a property because of its size or price, my wife would say to me, "wait a minute that location isn't very good" or highlight a problem with the listing that I overlooked, like Assessments for Water and Sewer that were not paid by the previous owner and will cost you thousands. When you both agree on the property as being the right one, then you need to have some financial tools to help you decide on what it will cost you and what income it can generate for you.

My financial tool was a spreadsheet that I could plug in numbers like purchase price, currency exchange, property taxes, insurance, down payment, mortgage or loan interest and see what the monthly costs would be. I could then compare those to the rental income I would estimate I needed to cover those costs. Have a look at my "Search Tools of the Trade" on page 86 for access to this financial tool.

Let me walk you through how I put this spreadsheet together then you will have a better idea on the power of such a tool. Don't worry about the spreadsheet formulas for now as I'll share those with you later.

First, you need to have a section in your spreadsheet to store and display the currency exchange. This can affect your purchase price and other one-time expenses needed at time of purchase. The example below shows Canadian currency close to parity with the US Dollar for a home price of USD $140,000.

	Input Fields are in Yellow	
Currency Exchange		
USD-CAD		1.010
CAD-USD		0.990
Purchase Price		
Home Price USD	$	140,000
Home Price CAD	$	141,400

However, that same home will cost you 10% more ($154,000) if the Canadian dollar moves back down to .90 cents per US Dollar. If you bought the home close to parity and the Canadian dollar slides back to .90 cents, then you've made a 10% capital gain (on paper anyways). I'm no economist but I believe there will be a spread again once the American engine starts firing on all cylinders and drawing down on their national debt and getting global foreign exchange (FX) currency stabilization. Barack Obama in his State of the Union address in January 2011 has already committed to driving down the national debt by $400 Billion in the next 5 years, so you can see that they are moving in the right direction with fiscal policy.

I use spreadsheets like Microsoft Excel (and Google spreadsheets) because spreadsheets contain built-in formulas for calculating interest payments on loans over a term. For example, I can setup an Excel worksheet (Tab in my Excel workbook) to show the payments made on a Mortgage for this house shown in the Table figure below.

Assume you make a 20% down payment ($28,000 on a $140,000 house). In Florida, if you tell the bank you are using the home as a vacation property, they will require 20% down payment. If you tell them you are buying it as an investment, they want 30%. With 20% down, you have 80% Loan-to-home-value (LTV) which is a standard FHA Loan (Federal Housing Administration) now part of the Department of Housing and Urban Development (HUD). FHA is like our CMHC (Canada Mortgage Housing Corporation) which insures loans below LTV ratios (In Canada – borrowing more than 75% of your home value) and protects the lender in case you, the borrower, defaults on the loan.

http://en.wikipedia.org/wiki/Federal_Housing_Administration

In the table shown below you will see a monthly payment of $615 (P+I). You can see how I made separate columns to show the changing Principal and Interest (P+I) payments for each pay Period (Per column). Based on a Term of 30 years (yes, Americans have terms that long), my interest rate will never change during that term, unless I renegotiate or re-finance (RE-FI).

USD	$ 222,017 Paid in	30.0 Years			$109,402	$112,615			
	Present Value	Rate	Per	Term	\	Interest	Principal	Acum Interest	Mortgage Insurance
2009 Jan	$ 112,000.00	5.20%	1	30	$ 615.00	$ 485.33	$ 129.67	$ 485.33	$ 69.44
Feb	$ 111,870.33	5.20%	2	30	$ 615.00	$ 484.77	$ 130.23	$ 970.10	$ 69.36
Mar	$ 111,740.10	5.20%	3	30	$ 615.00	$ 484.21	$ 130.80	$ 1,454.31	$ 69.28
Apr	$ 111,609.30	5.20%	4	30	$ 615.00	$ 483.64	$ 131.36	$ 1,937.95	$ 69.20
May	$ 111,477.94	5.20%	5	30	$ 615.00	$ 483.07	$ 131.93	$ 2,421.02	$ 69.12
Jun	$ 111,346.00	5.20%	6	30	$ 615.00	$ 482.50	$ 132.50	$ 2,903.52	$ 69.03
Jul	$ 111,213.50	5.20%	7	30	$ 615.00	$ 481.93	$ 133.08	$ 3,385.45	$ 68.95
Aug	$ 111,080.42	5.20%	8	30	$ 615.00	$ 481.35	$ 133.66	$ 3,866.80	$ 68.87
Sep	$ 110,946.76	5.20%	9	30	$ 615.00	$ 480.77	$ 134.23	$ 4,347.57	$ 68.79
Oct	$ 110,812.53	5.20%	10	30	$ 615.00	$ 480.19	$ 134.82	$ 4,827.75	$ 68.70
Nov	$ 110,677.71	5.20%	11	30	$ 615.00	$ 479.60	$ 135.40	$ 5,307.36	$ 68.62
Dec	$ 110,542.31	5.20%	12	30	$ 615.00	$ 479.02	$ 135.99	$ 5,786.37	$ 68.54
2010 Jan	$ 110,406.32	5.20%	13	30	$ 615.00	$ 478.43	$ 136.58	$ 6,264.80	$ 68.45
Feb	$ 110,269.75	5.20%	14	30	$ 615.00	$ 477.84	$ 137.17	$ 6,742.64	$ 68.37
Mar	$ 110,132.58	5.20%	15	30	$ 615.00	$ 477.24	$ 137.76	$ 7,219.88	$ 68.28
Apr	$ 109,994.81	5.20%	16	30	$ 615.00	$ 476.64	$ 138.36	$ 7,696.52	$ 68.20
May	$ 109,856.45	5.20%	17	30	$ 615.00	$ 476.04	$ 138.96	$ 8,172.57	$ 68.11
Jun	$ 109,717.49	5.20%	18	30	$ 615.00	$ 475.44	$ 139.56	$ 8,648.01	$ 68.02
Jul	$ 109,577.93	5.20%	19	30	$ 615.00	$ 474.84	$ 140.17	$ 9,122.85	$ 67.94
Aug	$ 109,437.77	5.20%	20	30	$ 615.00	$ 474.23	$ 140.77	$ 9,597.08	$ 67.85
Sep	$ 109,296.99	5.20%	21	30	$ 615.00	$ 473.62	$ 141.38	$ 10,070.70	$ 67.76
Oct	$ 109,155.61	5.20%	22	30	$ 615.00	$ 473.01	$ 142.00	$ 10,543.70	$ 67.68
Nov	$ 109,013.61	5.20%	23	30	$ 615.00	$ 472.39	$ 142.61	$ 11,016.10	$ 67.59
Dec	$ 108,871.00	5.20%	24	30	$ 615.00	$ 471.77	$ 143.23	$ 11,487.87	$ 67.50
2011 Jan	$ 108,727.77	5.20%	25	30	$ 615.00	$ 471.15	$ 143.85	$ 11,959.02	$ 67.41
Feb	$ 108,583.92	5.20%	26	30	$ 615.00	$ 470.53	$ 144.47	$ 12,429.56	$ 67.32
Mar	$ 108,439.45	5.20%	27	30	$ 615.00	$ 469.90	$ 145.10	$ 12,899.46	$ 67.23
Apr	$ 108,294.35	5.20%	28	30	$ 615.00	$ 469.28	$ 145.73	$ 13,368.74	$ 67.14
May	$ 108,148.62	5.20%	29	30	$ 615.00	$ 468.64	$ 146.36	$ 13,837.38	$ 67.05
Jun	$ 108,002.26	5.20%	30	30	$ 615.00	$ 468.01	$ 146.99	$ 14,305.39	$ 66.96
Jul	$ 107,855.26	5.20%	31	30	$ 615.00	$ 467.37	$ 147.63	$ 14,772.76	$ 66.87
Aug	$ 107,707.63	5.20%	32	30	$ 615.00	$ 466.73	$ 148.27	$ 15,239.49	$ 66.78

The next section of your spreadsheet should show the down payment and any one-time charges you'll need for closing the deal.

What are the one-time charges?

As you can see, the down payment plus the one-time charges need to come out of your savings. That means you should have $37,756 lying around somewhere. When you get a mortgage, the bank will want to know that you are not borrowing this down payment. So an equity line of credit (ELOC) won't help you.

These are fees and costs that your lender will charge for handling all the paperwork when buying a home. Make sure you are sitting down before reading this next section.

Down Payment		% PCT Down	$ AMT Down					
Enter in % or $ value		20%						
USD	$ 28,000	0%	Property Loan	One-Time Charges				TOTAL
CAD	$ 28,280		$ 28,280	$ 9,476	+	$ -		$ 37,756

ONE-TIME CHARGES			
USD Real Estate Transaction	$	275	Goes to R.E Office
USD Mortgage Application Fee	$	400	Goes to Bank
USD Lenders Fee	$	800	Goes to Bank
USD Escrow Settlement Fee	$	350	Goes to Bank
USD Lenders Title Insurance	$	25	Goes to Bank
USD Owners Title Insurance	$	900	Goes to Bank
USD Other Title Settlement Fees	$	209	Goes to Bank
USD Recording Fee	$	138	Goes to Bank
USD Tax Stamps	$	635	Goes to Bank
USD Survey	$	250	Goes to Bank
USD Closing Costs	$	2,100	1.50% of Purchase Price
USD Assessment (Sewer+Water)	$	-	Goes to City
USD Home Inspection	$	300	
USD Florida DOC Stamps	$	-	
USD Appliances	$	3,000	
USD Total	$	9,382	$ 9,476 <= Gets added

One-Time Charge	Fee Range	Explanation
Real Estate Transaction Fee	$200-$300	The Real Estate Broker charges an administration fee to prepare and process the paperwork. There's much debate about this fee but basically pays for the real estate office overhead to run a brokerage.
Mortgage Application Fee	$0-$500	This is the fee a lender may charge you for accepting the loan application. Remember, this fee is not refundable so be sure you want to deal with this lender before applying for a loan.
Lenders Processing Fee	$50-$250	The lender may pass on the cost of doing business to the borrower. This is the charge for processing the loan application. Sometimes called Lenders Document Preparation Fee. There's usually 60-70 pages involved with such loans given all the regulatory requirements for banks have to follow.
Lenders Credit Report Fees	$25-$60	There may be two credit reports pulled up on you and the co-borrower. The first one is pulled up when you apply for the loan and the second one may be pulled up just prior to closing.
Lenders Appraisal Fee	$300-$500	This is the fee the lender passes on to you for having the home appraised. Ideally, this should be the same amount the appraiser charged the lender for the service. There are also electronic appraisals, which search a huge database for price comparisons for homes that are similar to the one you are buying. The spreadsheet above shows the Lenders' Appraisal Fee, the Lenders' Processing Fee and the Credit Report Fee as one charge labeled as Lenders Fee.
Escrow Settlement Fee	$0-350	This is a fee paid one time to set up and service your property tax and Home Hazard Insurance costs from an escrow account where the bank settles this for you automatically and just adds the equal billing amount for these items to your mortgage payments.
Lenders Title Insurance	$50-$400	Title insurance protects the lender financially in the event somebody stakes a claim on the home you are purchasing. The cost of this insurance is passed on to you.
Owners Title Insurance	$3.65 per $1,000 of home appraisal amount	Title insurance is policy of indemnity protecting homeowners and lenders from financial loss in the event that certain problems develop regarding the rights to ownership of property. While closing attorneys check each title to real estate before a closing, there are often hidden title defects that even the most careful title search will not reveal. In addition to protection from financial loss, title insurance pays the cost of defending against any covered claim. There are two types of title insurance, lender's and owner's policies. Lender's policies are required by every public mortgage lender, but do not protect a property owner. Buyers must separately purchase an owner's policy.
Recording Fee	$6.00 min per page	This goes to the city or county you pay your property taxes. The Clerk's office charges a fee for the various services they perform, including a charge for recording, indexing and/or providing copies of deeds. While some counties may impose higher charges for recording documents, the following fees are the state-required minimums and are typical of most counties in Florida: $6.00 per page.
Document Tax Stamps	.007 x price of property	This goes to the city or county you pay your property taxes. Unless a transfer is exempted, Florida law provides that "the tax on deeds, instruments, documents or writings whereby any lands, tenements or other realty or any interest therein

		is transferred or conveyed is 70 cents on each $100 or fractional part thereof of the consideration paid". In plain English, this means that the documentary stamp tax is calculated in dollars to be 0.007 times the value of anything received in exchange for the transfer, with the value being rounded up to the next highest one hundred dollars. For example, if you deeded a piece of property to someone in exchange for payment of $9,970, the documentary stamp tax due would be $70.00 (10,000 x 0.007).

http://community.seattletimes.nwsource.com/reader_feedback/public/display.php?thread=19142&offset=0#post_88786
http://www.relocation.com/library/mortgage_guide/mortgage_fees.html
http://www.boston.com/realestate/news/blogs/renow/2009/08/title_insurance_1.html
http://www.marioncountyclerk.org/public/index.cfm?Pg=feescalculator
http://www.southptc.com/florida-closing-cost-calculator.html

Land Survey	$150-$350	This will be needed for the mortgage and Insurance and may include a Flood Certificate which species the elevation of the base floor of your property.
Closing Costs	1.5%	The closing costs are typically 1.5% of the home purchase price or $1,500 per $100,000.
Assessments	$0 and up	These are impact fees due when the property was connected to city water/sewer.
Home Inspection Fee	$250-$350	The home inspection is voluntary but highly recommended if you are buying a house on a FAR-BAR AS-IS contract. It will allow you to back out of the deal if you uncover significant repairs.
Appliances	$600-$3,000	Appliances are not always included in the sale of the home. In fact, you need to look carefully at the MLS Listing to see what's included. Also make sure "pool equipment stays" is stated.

Now that you have figured out the down payment and one-time charges for yourself you are on your way to preventing any surprise lump sum charges that could make you queasy. Remember that you are just doing your due diligence to ensure that you have taken everything into consideration before you make your financial decision. Like I said, this exercise can really temper your emotion for jumping too soon.

Mortgage Payments

USD **Mortgage Amount**	$ 112,000	**113,120**				
USD **Amortization (Years)**	30.0					
USD **Interest Rate**	5.200%					
USD **Interest (Month)**	$ 485			**Does your RENT cover the Mortgage Payments ?**		
USD **Principal (Month)**	$ 130	**Annual**		Yes	$ 154.75	Extra Left Over
USD **Property Taxes (Month)**	$ 233	$ 2,800				each month
USD **Insurance (Flood)**	$ 38	$ 459				and applied to
USD **Insurance (Dwelling)**	$ 40	$ 477				US Mortgage
USD **Insurance (Hurricane)**	$ 29	$ 349				
USD **Insurance (Liability)**	$ 15	$ 178				
	$ -					
USD **TOTAL (Monthly)**	$ 970	$ 11,643	$ 222,017 paid over	30.0 Years		

EXPENSES

USD **Electricity**	$ -	
USD **Water**	$ -	
USD **Pool Maintenance**	$ 60	$ 720
USD **Property Maintenance**	$ 75	$ 900
USD **Property Management**	$ -	
USD **Lawn & Tree Fertilization**	$ 45	$ 540
USD **Total Monthly Expenses**	$ 180	$ 2,160

ANNUAL RENTAL

USD **Rental (Month)**	$ 1,125	$ 13,500

This next section above builds on the previous sections and shows you what the monthly mortgage will cost you when also factoring in Property Taxes, Insurance. As you can see from above section, your monthly commitments to the bank, assuming you pay your property taxes and insurance from an Escrow account, is $970 per month. Assuming you get a minimum of $970 per month rent, you will show a positive cash flow for the property which would cover your Mortgage and Insurance expenses.

However, when you factor in other expenses that you may need, like Pool and Lawn Maintenance, you will need to ask for higher rent if you want to have those fees covered. You would need $1,150 ($970 + $180) to have your rent cover all expenses. That means the property can carry the operating expenses. However, you may have overlooked the $37,756 of your own money for the down payment and one-time charges.

For this property to be truly cash flow positive, you should factor in the monthly cost of that down payment spread over your term (30 years). Since you didn't borrow the down payment (because you are not allowed to, as banks want you to have that money in cash) you just simply divide the down payment and one-time charges over the number of payments for a 30 year term (30 * 12 = 360 payments) which ends up being $104.

Having a cash flow positive property is wonderful, but it might not work out for you in all cases. This will be a decision on whether you feel the investment will pay back over time as rental prices will increase, or your costs may decrease, or you are betting the value of your home will go up to cover that shortfall over the years. For example, you could disregard the down payment costs ($37,756) if you think after 30 years your property will be worth today's price ($140,000) plus that amount for a new selling price of $177,756. Remember to deduct Real Estate commissions of 5% on average as the Seller and you would fetch $168,868 for your home which is a 21% gain over 30 years. That's very attainable. A 10-year US Government Bond right now pays 2.5% yield.

What will rent be in 30 years from now? Nobody can tell you with absolute certainty but inflation is usually more of a threat than deflation. The US Federal Reserve is always working to *avoid* deflation (economy contraction) and *control* inflation (economy expansion). That means your rental income should be going up by inflationary terms (today, that's 0.5% per year compounded annually - table shown on right). In my experience, if you keep the rent fixed year over year, once you change it, your tenants may become surprised and start shopping for another place, creating tenant churn for yourself. If you have good tenants, that's worth money you don't have to spend, finding new ones. Establish your policy early and stick with it. Either charge high enough rent that will cover all your expenses which may take a bit longer to find tenants willing to pay or specify in your lease contract that you automatically increase rent every year by a certain percentage.

YEAR	RENT	0.5%
1	$ 900.00	$ 4.50
2	$ 904.50	$ 4.52
3	$ 909.02	$ 4.55
4	$ 913.57	$ 4.57
5	$ 918.14	$ 4.59
6	$ 922.73	$ 4.61
7	$ 927.34	$ 4.64
8	$ 931.98	$ 4.66
9	$ 936.64	$ 4.68
10	$ 941.32	$ 4.71
11	$ 946.03	$ 4.73
12	$ 950.76	$ 4.75
13	$ 955.51	$ 4.78
14	$ 960.29	$ 4.80
15	$ 965.09	$ 4.83
16	$ 969.91	$ 4.85
17	$ 974.76	$ 4.87
18	$ 979.64	$ 4.90
19	$ 984.54	$ 4.92
20	$ 989.46	$ 4.95
21	$ 994.41	$ 4.97
22	$ 999.38	$ 5.00
23	$1,004.37	$ 5.02
24	$1,009.40	$ 5.05
25	$1,014.44	$ 5.07
26	$1,019.52	$ 5.10
27	$1,024.61	$ 5.12
28	$1,029.74	$ 5.15
29	$1,034.89	$ 5.17
30	$1,040.06	$ 5.20

You may be tempted to reduce your costs and save by not having to pay for pool care and lawn care if your tenant agrees to perform these duties. However, you'll normally have to compensate your tenants with reduced rent. I can say from experience, that it's best to have professionals take care of your property. If you are not happy with the services, you can terminate the company services and look for someone else. You can't do that with your tenant. Besides, your tenant will serve as your eyes and ears as custodians of your property and they will tell you if the services are not being performed properly. That will alert you to contacting the company to find out what is going on or to find a new one.

On the question of affordability, if you don't have the down payment lying around, how could you even consider buying some property? Do you have any equity in your current home? If you do, then you may want to consider getting an Equity Line of Credit (ELOC) and paying for the home with a *Cash-Offer*. Your offer will be more attractive to sellers. The only thing you will need from your bank is a "Proof of Funds" letter which basically states you have the funds available to you to use towards the purchase of a property. Then after you own the own, go to TD Bank in the USA to get financing on your new second home. They will lend you up to 80% of the value of the home. Take that money they lend you and pay off your ELOC.

If you have some funds you can tap into for the down payment, such as some investments that are not performing as you liked then it's still better to try and get a mortgage in the USA if possible. The next section on, "What are your Financing Options" on page 38 gives you some more ideas.

So you hate to pay banks all those fees. Remember that the fees are one-time charges at purchase time only. However, if you want to save the Closing Costs (1.5% of home price) and all the Lender fees noted above, you can come in with your own money which is considered a *Cash-Offer* and usually more competitive than financed offers.

Consider these two scenarios when deciding between USA and Canadian borrowed money:

1. Get a US mortgage rate at 5.2% over 30 years, your interest payments are $485 per month
2. Get a Canadian mortgage at 8.25% over 25 years, your interest payments are $770 per month

That's a difference of $285 every month. Most of those bank fees were close to that figure. That means each month the difference would end up paying for each of these fees. After many months, you'd be in the clear. There's one other fee you should look into. That is buying down your interest rate with points (explained in "What are your Financing Options" on page 38). This too will save you money over the long term. It usually pays for itself with 2-3 years, and if you are holding for the long term it won't really matter. The USA mortgage rates are at historic lows (may not be seen again in decades).

What are your Financing Options

As of 2009, most USA banks have stopped lending to foreign nationals as they have pulled back from the Mortgage Subprime crisis to deal with the flood of Foreclosures and Short Sales and REFIs (refinancing) that home owners are coming to them with.

I have a mortgage with Bank of America on one of my properties and I can tell you from personal experience it was like a nightmare to prove to them where the money was coming from for the down payment. It took close to 60 days of back and forth emails, document signing, going in person to Buffalo, NY bank branches to prove my identity (new with 9/11 Patriot Act) that I would not want to subject myself to that ever again.

However, RBC Bank USA provides USA Mortgages for Canadians. The link below will help you find a Mortgage specialist to start discussing how you can get pre-approved.

http://mortgage.rbcbankusa.com/   or

http://www.rbcbankusa.com/specialtybanking/cid-96799.html

Another Canadian Bank that can provide USA Mortgages for Canadians is TD Bank and was my best experience.

http://tdbank.mortgagewebcenter.com/CheckRates/SearchCriteria.asp?PID=22

Why get a USA Mortgage? The main reason is your ability to lock in a Mortgage rate to a Fixed 30 Year Term. As an investor, you want predictable costs as much as possible. If you have calculated a positive cash flow property, the last thing you want is to renew your term at new market rates. Renewing your term at new higher rates will destroy your financial model for positive cash flow and send more of your rental income to paying off the bank loan.

Remember that I'm talking about the Term and not Amortization. The Amortization of the loan calculates the number of payments towards Principal in order to pay off the loan for that Amortization period (i.e. 30 years).

The Mortgage Term re-adjusts your Interest payments higher or lower over the Term period (i.e. 5 years). If the Amortization stays the same, then only your Interest payments change but it will affect your monthly payment amount. The Term is what actually determines how much more you end up paying for your property over the life of the loan (Amortization period).

The longest Fixed Rate Mortgage (also called a Closed Mortgage) in Canada is a 10 year fixed rate term.

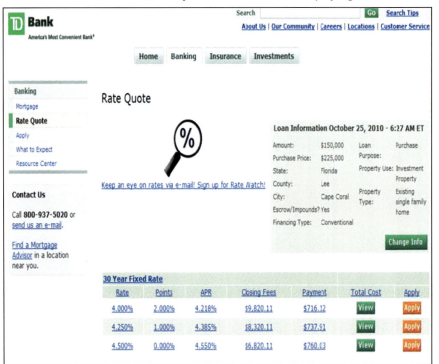

TD Bank and Bank of Montreal offered these mortgages at 5.09% and 6.85% respectively. The only bank I found that offers a longer mortgage term was Royal Bank of Canada. It offers a 25 year Fixed Rate Mortgage at 8.25%. In the USA, a Bank of America offers a 30 Year Fixed Term at 4.5%.

If you are getting a mortgage with a USA Bank, like Bank of America, they will charge a premium on the Interest rates because we are *Foreign Nationals* (http://en.wikipedia.org/wiki/Foreign_national). That's if you can find a bank to lend to you. As *Foreign Nationals* we are considered higher risk (go figure that one out). TD Bank does not do this so I recommend staying with them.

Banks will offer you the ability to pay down the Interest rate by as much as half a percent. They call it buying down with points (up to a maximum of 2 points where 1 point = 0.25% interest). Each point costs 1% of your loan amount. For example, if you want to borrow $180,000 and the interest rate is 4.50% and you wanted to lock in a rate of 4.00%, you could pay $3,600 up front to discount that rate (1% of $180,000 = $1,800 or $3,600 for 2 point discount).

Other fees you need to be aware of are closing costs.

TD Bank does a good job on their website of showing you all the fees and costs and the cash you'll need at closing as shown on the right.

The $400 appraisal fee is for the bank to determine the value of the home. They will use their own Real Estate Broker to determine the market value and comparable properties through a BPO (Broker Price Opinion). A property might be listed for $225,000 and you offer $215,000 for it, but the bank tells you that in their opinion it's only worth $200,000. If you are putting down 20%, then you are borrowing 80%. The bank is providing 80% Loan-to-Value (LTV). They will only lend you 80% of the $200,000 (not $225,000).

Is that bad? No, that's good; it's giving you a chance to send back a revised offer based on market value of the home. Will the seller accept? They might if they recognize that you wanted the home but your bank is stopping you and giving you an independent 3rd party opinion on its market true value. It takes some emotion out of the negotiation, which is always good.

Total Cost Assumptions		
Annual Real Estate Taxes:		$3,800
Estimated Closing Date:		11/15/2010
		Change Info

Total Cost:		
Purchase Price		**$225,000.00**
TD Bank's origination charge		$368.45
Your charge for this interest rate		$0.00
Required services we select		$475.66
Appraisal Fee	$400.00	
Credit Report	$10.96	
Customer Authentication Report	$1.70	
Flood Determination	$5.00	
Tax Related Service Fee	$58.00	
Title services and lender's title insurance		$1,975.00
Owner's title insurance		$1,350.00
Government recording charges		$251.00
Transfer taxes		$2,400.00
Initial escrow deposit		$1,360.44
Daily interest charges		$536.30
Homeowners insurance		$562.56
Hazard Insurance Premium	$562.56	
Your new loan amount		($150,000.00)
Estimated Cash Required at Closing		**$84,279.41**

This happened to me. The house was offered at $220,000, there were other offers and I over bid to get the property at $233,500. The bank appraised it at $220,000. I sent the offer back, to the lowered $220,000. By that time, all other buyers have gone away being told they were out bid. It takes at least 5-10 days to have this appraisal done as banks move slowly. By that time, it was their only offer on the property. They accepted the lower $220,000. So the $400 appraisal fee is worth your protection and saved me $13,500.

They will do a credit check on your financial history plus a few other checks like Flood Determination which is to look at where your property sits in terms of Flood zones. The bulk of the charges are in Title Search and Land Transfer Taxes. Title searches ensure the property was always in legal possession and not involved in any fraud related activities. It ensures free and clear title to the property once purchased and provides the bank with insurance against all such claims coming to them afterwards since they own most of the house when they hold the mortgage.

The escrow account can be setup with the bank to have them pay your Property taxes and Home Hazard Insurance. Normally this service is provided at no additional charge by the bank but requires you to deposit an initial amount which they will estimate for you at time of closing. It's a good thing to help you budget for fixed monthly payments to the bank.

Another reason to get a mortgage is leverage.

You can use all of your cash to purchase a home or you can use your cash to pay the minimal down payment on two or more homes and borrow the rest. That's leverage. It's really up to you on your comfort level but remember that your borrowing charges are tax deductible expenses. You really don't get rewarded for using your own cash to invest in something by our own government. However, you do get rewarded for carrying costs over a term and claiming those costs to reduce your tax burden. You may not want more than one home but the cash you didn't have to tie up into Florida real estate could be directed to other asset classes like Stocks, Bonds, Gold or GICs for a balanced and more diversely allocated investment portfolio.

I want you to be aware of how Florida home prices are set versus Canadian home prices. In Canada the home price is set to what the seller thinks they can get as a maximum amount for their home. For a Canadian home listed on the Multiple Listing Service (MLS) offers will come in up to 100% and sometimes in rare multiple offer situations over 100%.

In Florida, the prices in this market right now are usually set as the starting bid price. That means the sellers recognize their homes are in competition with many homes in foreclosure or short sale and some regular sales. They purposely set the price low to attract offers and expect multiple offers to drive up the price. If the house and price seem too good to be true, then you know that this is the starting bid and expect many other offers.

You can probably expect to overbid by as much as 10% over the asking price if you want to be a competitive bid. You might be asked to submit your best and final offer if numerous buyers are involved. If that happens, just remember what happened to me and let your home appraisal be your opportunity to re-approach he seller to reduce it to the appraisal value if it's lower than your best and final offer.

Insurance

There are 4 types of Insurance you should consider as part of your investment protection:

1. Home Hazard Insurance
2. Flood Insurance (FEMA)
3. Hurricane Insurance
4. Umbrella Liability Insurance

Home Hazard Insurance is usually referred to as damage caused by Fire, Theft, Vandalism or Lightning strikes. My premiums run me about $1200 per year for full cost replacement. Let me tell you what I learned about having full replacement cost.

If you get a large Hurricane sweeping through your neighborhood and 100 homes get damage, your claim for repairs will be one in many. There will be tradespeople or companies to repair your damaged home. Although it is illegal practice, supplies like lumber, roof tiles, windows will be in high demand but in short supply. There's a risk of the prices for these materials to go substantially higher, sometimes double or triple. Also labour rates could increase.

Quote Summary
The rates are not guaranteed and may change at anytime.

Quote Number: 9022FL 00C2969

Applicant Information:
Michael Geraats
Risk Location:
1529 Sw 52nd St
Cape Coral FL 33914   Lee County

Agency Information:
Today's Ins Solutions, P.a.
10524 Moss Park Rd Ste 204-249
Orlando, FL 32832
407-982-1200

Date Quoted: 5/22/2009	Form Type: DP-3	Plan Type: Standard
Effective Date: 6/22/2009	Expiration Date: 6/22/2010	

Rating/Underwriting Information:

Construction Type: Masonry		Month/Year Built: 01/1981
Territory Code: 554-Lee - remainder		Protection Class: 03
BCEG 99		Protection Device Credit: 0
Named Hurricane Ded: 2% of Coverage A		All Other Perils Ded: $1000 Deductible
		Shape of Roof: Hip Roof

Coverages:	Limit	Premium
Coverage A. Dwelling:	$205,000	$923.00
Coverage B. Other Structures	$2,050	Incl.
Coverage D. Fair Rental Value	$20,500	Incl.
Coverage L. Liability	$300,000	$80.00
Coverage M. Med Pay	$5,000	Incl.
Other Endorsement Premium		$100.00
Subtotal:		$1,103.00
MGA Policy Fee		$25.00
Emergency Management Trust Fund Surcharge		$2.00
Estimated Total Premium		**$1,130.00**

*The quoted premium is an estimated premium based on information obtained at this time. Premium may differ based on information obtained on final application.

Suppliers know they can get a higher price because the cost will be passed on to insurance companies to pay. Full replacement cost ensures your home gets rebuilt at today's prices (not based on a depreciated value). If I get a fire which destroys my house, my deductible is $1000. If it is destroyed by a Hurricane, my deductible is 2% of coverage, which in this case is limited to **Coverage A. Dwelling** ($205,000) or $4,000 for my home to be rebuilt.

You should also make sure you have **Fair Rental Value**. If your house is damaged, or even as little as broken windows where the A/C won't be able to keep the house cool for your tenants, your insurance company will pay for your tenants to live somewhere else until repairs are complete. The above example shows they will pay up to $20,500 for their accommodation (rent for more than a year) and up to $5,000 for their medical fees (**Coverage M. Med Pay**) in case they got hurt during a storm.

If you are being sued for *gross negligence*, then the **Coverage L. Liability** item covers up to $300,000 worth of legal fees. However, I always recommend an **Umbrella Liability Policy** which will increase that coverage to $1,000,000. The annual premium is $178 but will add   additional coverage to *all* your properties (Umbrella policy).

Nail Spacing 6/6 8d

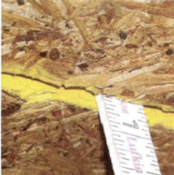

Do you want to bring down your Home Insurance premium? Then get a Wind Mitigation study done. It is a report on how well your home would fare in high hurricane winds and what are the probabilities for damage.

They check your roof, how the rafters are secured, nail spacing and type of truss wraps that will prevent your roof from pulling off in severe Category 5 Hurricanes (155 mile per hour winds). It costs about $125 to get the study done, but depending on the home age, will save you many times that amount in premiums. The newer your home, the better chances for discounts.
By the way, you cannot get a mortgage or close on a property until you have Home Insurance.

There are other Insurance Mitigation policies you can get for Radon Mitigation and Sink Hole protection. I did not go crazy trying to insure for everything and therefore declined coverage.

Flood insurance is mandatory in Florida and the Federation Emergency Management Agency (FEMA) mandates you to have this Insurance. The premiums for my properties range from $450-$750 and depend on your Flood Elevation Certificate which you need before getting FEMA Insurance. It basically wants to know what Flood Zone you live in and then what is the elevation level of your ground floor. There are no basements for Florida homes, unlike Canadian homes, so that means your main or ground level floor.

Hurricane insurance as mentioned is usually covered in your Home Hazard Policy. I learned a lot about Hurricanes as I spent more time in Florida. A Hurricane is really a wind pressure phenomenon. It will find the weakest pressure point on your house and potentially exploit it. For example, most access doors to the roof or attic are through a door in your garage ceiling (sometimes with a drop down ladder). Many older garage doors are made of corrugated sheet metal. If a Category 5 Hurricane throws an object against your metal garage door, your door could take a significant hit and become compromised. Your garage door may now have a slight opening where wind will force its way into your garage. As that happens the opening will become larger and it would find its way upwards towards your roof through your attic door. Once that happens, it creates a vortex and could then pull your roof off your house.

The simple solution is to ensure your garage door has cross beam metal beams screwed on to prevent any buckling. Then also secure your attic door with metal rebar, prevent it from pulling up into the attic. I've seen homes reinforced this way.

What about windows when they become compromised? The new Hurricane Impact Resistant windows are built to Miami-Dade Building Code (http://www.hurricane.com/hurricane-impact-windows.php) level. The Miami-Dade Building Code specifies that a window is able to withstand a 2x4 lumber stud hurdling at it at 50 feet per second without penetrating it. So you want to go replace all your windows? They are about 2-3 times more expensive than your double glazed window. I also found out that your Insurance does not go down enough to recoup the costs for such windows. The simple solution is to get Hurricane shutters. They are corrugated sheet metal that goes over your window to protect any objects from penetrating the glass and creating a hole into your house, which would lead to further damage.

If you want to replace any window in your house and you are not using Impact Resistant windows, you are limited to replacing only 25% of the window pane area over your entire house. If you have 100 square feet of window pane, then only 25 square feet are permitted for replacement each year. If you are replacing with impact resistant windows, then there are no restrictions other than your budget.

Estate Taxes, Incorporating and Cross Border Trusts

There's a whole lot of information on this topic but the best place to start is perhaps visit http://www.altrolaw.com to see what is involved when buying property and holding title to it from another country, like Canada. The USA laws are different and many of those laws don't recognize Canadian laws on Probate, Estate Taxes, Shared Ownership like putting the names of your Children on the property and situations when one of you are under Power of Attorney, such as Dementia or in a coma.

Once investors get engaged into this market, many will ask the big question. That is, "Should I setup a corporation or holding company to shield my assets in the event of litigation and separate them from my personal wealth?"

The answer depends on what you want. A corporation cannot get a Mortgage on a property. A corporation will save on income Taxes because you pay corporate tax and not personal income tax. However, when it comes time to sell your assets (properties) you will pay close to 35% Federal Estate Taxes and about 5% Florida state taxes. You also cannot apply any losses on the property to your personal income situation because the corporation is its own entity. Remember rule #1 on why to invest in Florida is to reduce your income taxes by offsetting your personal income with investment expenses.

Another great idea people will have to avoid probate taxes is to put the name of your children on their property deed. The problem with that approach is that the IRS (Internal Revenue Service) will see your children as the beneficiary of this property as a "Gift" and will apply their rules in the form of a "Gift Tax". Unless you can prove they paid into the property through receipts for transactions of their own personal income, it will be difficult to claim them as heirs or beneficiaries to your property.

What happens when you put the names of your children on the trust and they in turn get married and then divorced one day. Their spouse is legally entitled to 50% of that property and may trigger a tax situation you didn't anticipate.

What happens when the name of your child on your property claims bankruptcy? The bankruptcy courts will find property in their name and creditors may come to claim for a disposition of that property in order to settle the debts owed.

What happens when your spouse is unable to make a decision or sign control over to you to sell the property? Perhaps they are in a Coma or have Alzheimer's or somehow declared unfit by the courts to rule on their own behalf. The Canadian courts will recognize Power of Attorney or Living Wills if you have one, but the US courts don't.

How do you avoid such situations? Establish or setup a Cross Border Trust (CBT) which can help shield you and your children from such adverse tax laws across the border. It costs roughly $5,000 but can save you thousands depending on your situation and how much property you own.

Property Taxes

There are large misconceptions about Property Taxes on Florida properties. As Canadians, we certainly pay our fair share of taxes so we are sensitive to high taxes.

Only 41 states impose state income taxes (http://retirementliving.com/RLtaxes.html) and Florida is not one of those states. Florida collects taxes through other means like property tax and sales tax (6% on most items except food, clothing and prescription drugs).

Property taxes are calculated the same way that most Canadian municipalities calculate them and that's through levies based on mill rates applied to the property based on its *assessed value*, which is almost always lower than the market value. The advantage for USA citizens owning a home is that they get to reduce the *assessed value* by $25,000 per person listed on the deed of the property. There are two state programs called Homestead Exemption and SOH - Save Our Homes (http://www.davidsporleder.com/blog/the-abcs-of-florida-homestead-exemption-and-save-our-homes.html) where USA citizens are given an advantage over foreign nationals buying up real estate.

Here's how the Homestead Exemption works. If you have a Florida Driver's License with Florida Vehicle License plates on at least one car, proof of United States Citizenship, Social Security Number and your Florida home is your primary residence then you will qualify for up to a $50,000 deduction on the *county assessed value* of your home.

For example if the house is assessed at $150,000, then you are eligible to reduce the assessed value down by $25,000 per person. These property taxes would then be based on the reduced assessed value of $100,000 (less $25,000 for each person assuming a couple) and would obviously result in a lower property tax bill.

The Save of Homes Amendment (SOH) limits property tax increases by 3% tax increase limitation on annual assessments. If you qualify for standard Home Exemption then you automatically qualify for "Save Our Homes" limitation.

As the owner of four Florida properties, my property tax bill for a home I bought in a really nice area of Cape Coral (South West region) for $140,000 is about $2,263 per year. My Gulf Access properties (with pools) I pay almost double that amount ($4,250 per year). Having a Gulf Access property means direct access to the Gulf of Mexico from your backyard with a sailboat or Yacht. Imagine the property taxes you would pay for a home backing onto Lake Ontario, Vancouver Island, PEI or Cape Breton Island.

Of course, property taxes depend on many things, like location, size of home, assessed value of home. My point is to demonstrate that property taxes should not deter you from buying any real estate. It is just another expense that is calculated when you crunch your numbers to determine if your rental income will cover those costs.

So where is the threat of property taxes? As a Canadian you will not qualify for Home Exemption or SOH. Therefore, if property home prices start to skyrocket, then so will your assessed value, and your property taxes will follow. It comes down to your belief in whether property prices will increase dramatically and bounce back or will it be more slow and gradual.

With the amount of foreclosures, short sales and home auctions that have hit the nation, not just Florida, property price increases will be slow and gradual as the new normal. I would say that this Great Recession will not be forgotten anytime soon. About 20% of Americans have lost their homes to Foreclosure by a bank and will have a bankruptcy claim on their credit file that will stay there for 7 years. Banks will be reluctant to lend to those folks that have Foreclosed on a property until their credit score is restored.

Remember the goal. Invest now, to get a foot hold into the market. Later on it's your decision, turn the properties into vacation rentals or sell them at a substantial profit and redirect those funds into something else that drives your passion. It all depends on your individual situation. Perhaps you will like the passive income of a Vacation Rental during retirement or perhaps you want to take up the art of wine making in the South of France and get a little place there instead.

How do I file my Income Tax

Your income taxes are processed the same way as if you owned real estate in Canada. Once major difference is that instead of using Canadian Rental property addresses, you will list USA property addresses as part of your CRA (Canada Revenue Agency) T776(E) taxation forms.

However, you will also need to make the IRS (Internal Revenue Service) aware of your foreign owned property by filing with the USA taxation system. Therefore, you'll need a Canadian Tax Accountant and a USA Tax Account or CPA (Chartered Professional Account). Remember that the fees you pay to these professionals are tax deductible.

The Canadian deadline for Tax submissions is April 30 and the USA deadline is June 15 of each calendar year.

As part of your filing with the IRS in the USA, you will need to file a W-8BEN Form (Certificate of Foreign Status of Beneficial Owner for United States Tax Withholding) - http://www.irs.gov/pub/irs-pdf/fw8ben.pdf.

The W-8BEN form exempts withholding taxes for Canadians upon disposition or the sale of any properties in the USA. If you don't file this form, the default withholding tax for Canada is 30%. That means the government will hold back 30% of your sale of goods until you file your taxes and declare you are a Foreign Beneficial Owner.

As part of filing your taxes for the first time you will need to file a W-7 form with the USA government (Application for IRS Individual Taxation Identification Number) - http://www.irs.gov/pub/irs-pdf/fw7.pdf.

The W-7 is used to assign you an ITIN (Individual Taxpayer Identification Number). Although it looks like a SSN (Social Security Number) and has the same number of digits as an SSN (xxx-xx-xxxx), it is used to identify, register and track your financial affairs in the USA as a Non-Resident Alien.

Another form you will need to file with the IRS is a 1040NR (U.S Non-Resident Alien Income Tax Return) - http://www.irs.gov/pub/irs-pdf/i1040nr.pdf. Basically you are going to tally your income and expenses, same Canadian form T776 and report an income or loss on your form.

Income:		Properties A	B	C		Totals (Add columns A, B, and C)
3 Rents received	3	5,700.	4,125.	4,208.	3	14,033.
4 Royalties received	4				4	
Expenses:						
5 Advertising	5		88.	69.		
6 Auto and travel (see instructions)	6	644.	1,005.	1,010.		
7 Cleaning and maintenance	7					
8 Commissions	8					
9 Insurance	9	835.	2,039.	1,837.		
10 Legal and other professional fees	10	406.	50.	277.		
11 Management fees	11	256.	188.	248.		
12 Mortgage interest paid to banks, etc (see instructions)	12	4,204.	1,934.	1,422.	12	7,560.
13 Other interest	13					
14 Repairs	14		3,344.	4,129.		
15 Supplies	15					
16 Taxes	16	1,150.	1,240.	996.		
17 Utilities	17		130.	200.		
18 Other (list) ▶ Office expense			35.	24.	275.	
	18					

Buying Short Sales and Foreclosures

First some terminology and explanation on what a Short Sale or Foreclosure is.

A Short Sale is the process whereby the borrower (home owner) negotiates with the lender (bank) for reduced monthly payments due to financial hardship. There's no obligation for the lender to agree to any such arrangement since they have a binding legal contract that states the borrower owes them a certain amount of money for the home. The alternative is for the borrower to walk away from the obligation and declare bankruptcy. That situation is not ideal for either party. The borrower loses the equity they paid into owning the home for the time they did and being saddled with a bankruptcy on their credit file. The bank also loses as it costs them for all the paperwork and legal work needed to send this home into Foreclosure, where they reclaim ownership of the asset and place it back on the market for re-sale.

Short Sales can take months for the negotiations between borrower and lender to be worked out. During the mortgage sub-prime crisis (2008-2009) the banks were under staffed and overwhelmed with the flood of defaults happening. It was taking between 9-18 months to process short sales and foreclosures. Today, that has improved dramatically and is taking about 3-4 months on average. If you find a Short Sale property you love, and it's listed for $150,000, that price can represent the seller's price. It doesn't mean the bank has agreed to that price, unless it states that in the MLS (Multiple Listing Service) description for that property. Your real estate agent can usually guide you and find out what the situation is. The nice thing about Short Sales is that you can put in an offer and if you find something else, you can withdraw your offer. The other nice thing is that you don't have to put down any escrow funds to support 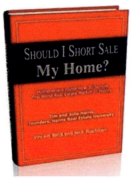 your offer (In the USA is sometimes "*earnest money*") until it is accepted. That means you can shop, put in your offers, and wait to see what comes back.

A Foreclosure is a bank owned home. The previous home owners have defaulted on their mortgage payments for many months with opportunity to pay but didn't. They were sent a letter stating that the bank is foreclosing on the home loan and taking back ownership. The process for buying a Foreclosure is much shorter than a Short Sale and could be anywhere from 1 month to 2 months. Most real estate agents will steer you to Foreclosures or regular sales for obvious reasons, they want to make sales and not wait for many, many months. I would not rule them out only because you can make offers without any commitment, and see what happens. In real estate, anything can happen, so it's good to have options open to you.

One thing I noticed is that if a home price seems too low, or too good to be true, it usually means a starting price. In Canada, it is usually the opposite where homes are listed for the maximum price the seller feels they could get for the property and settles for a price something below asking. In my experience, the banks have been putting out the Foreclosed homes back on the market for a very low price and getting multiple offers. So, you are sometimes bidding in a blind auction with opportunities to increase your bid. Personally, I hate auctions and usually feel that I'm paying too much in the end.

My recommendation for this situation is to make your offer *on condition of financing*. This means that a bank needs to appraise your home and tell you how much they will loan you based on the appraisal. For example, if you put an offer of $165,000 on a home listed for $150,000 you are over bidding and may win the bid. Once you win the bid, have your bank to appraise the home as part of the mortgage process. This usually takes a week or longer. By that time all the other bidders have been told they lost out to a winning bid. Once your bank comes back to tell you that the house has been appraised at $155,000, then you can send that back to the listing agent requesting a reduction of your bid to accept $155,000. It's a dirty trick and has no guarantees of working but will allow you to escape the deal if they don't accept your reduced offer because you made your offer on condition of financing. That means they need to contact the next highest bidder to see if they are still interested. In the heat of bidding, people lose their rational thoughts and asking the bidder to come back after they have time to cool off and think about it or perhaps realize there are other deals out there, they may not respond. Now you are in the power position. It may or may not work, but my point here is to know this when you go into any multiple offer scenario.

Your best chances will come when you have done enough research and shopping to know what is a good deal and what is not. Remember, you also have an agent that you will work with to be your guide and supporter. However, I would not rely on your agent alone to help you with your final decision. It needs to make financial sense for your goal. I help you with that part in the section entitled, Search Tools of the Trade on page 86.

Your Property Search

You will find numerous property search tools on the internet to help you find your ideal property. I listed many of the ones I used in "Search Tools of the Trade" on page 86.

Getting a list of available properties for sale is only the beginning. How do you know what's a good deal? In order to answer this question you will require a higher level of proficiency with those search tools. For example, is there a feature that allows you to list the recently sold properties in that area to show you what homes or condos are selling for? Normally, your real estate agent will be able to "run the comps" (comparable listings) for you to tell you what's good value comparatively, but I always like to know myself.

If you are planning to rent, what are properties in that area, for that size home or condo renting for? Many search engine tools also have rental listing features. Wouldn't you want to know potential rental income before committing to a mortgage or loan to buy the property?

Also, what are the property taxes and how do you find out? Property taxes could kill your financial model and they fluctuate. In Florida, property taxes have been coming down over the years, but when the market improves, they'll start going back up again, once the city and municipalities alter the mill rates. One of the tools I use is Property Appraiser site for the county you are buying in. For example, if I'm buying a property in Lee County, I do a Google search for Lee County Property Appraiser. These sites are provided by the city and will therefore usually end in .org as part of the internet address domain name. In this case, it would be http://www.leepa.org. One of my favorite features is the aerial viewer with overlays. You could use Google Maps with Street View to drive through the neighborhood, but the overlays that you can check off on the right allow you to see property boundaries, the market value, or last price sold on the homes in the neighborhood. This can be valuable information.

These sites provide enormous amounts of free and accessible information (as part of FOIP – Freedom of Information Act/Program) that will prove invaluable to you making a sound financial decision. It will for example list for you the following types of information:

a) Names of the current owners for that property
b) What they paid for the property and in what year
c) The names of all previous owners of this property and what they paid for it before selling it
d) Documents they signed (in PDF format)
e) Tax Roll information for current year and all prior years
f) Property Assessments still outstanding and owed to the city for converting to City Water and Sewer
g) Any outstanding permits or liens against the property
h) Pictures of the property for each taxation year (GIS Geographic Information System with Aerial Photography)
i) Land and Building sizes with overview diagrams of square footage for each area and lot size
j) Distance drawing tools (see below how I measured the neighbors' pool enclosure area (shows 1121 SqFt).

The list goes on and on and has very useful information that will help you get a sense of what your property has.

One of the things I look at is the sale transaction history. This is what tells me what the market was willing to pay in a peak market scenario. Although I don't expect markets to reach the peak sale prices soon, real estate is a cyclical system just like the stock market, and it usually trends upwards or downwards as it chops up and down. World real estate prices have gone upwards everywhere. Consider Saskatchewan where few people felt there was a robust lifestyle other than wheat farming. It's like saying I'm moving to Nebraska. However, real estate prices in Saskatchewan have soared. The reason is that many could not afford the prices of homes in nearby Calgary or Edmonton in Alberta. Young families need to start where they can afford to live. The British are buying up more properties in Romania, Bulgaria and Turkey since Spain, France and Italy prices have soared with their recent invasion of Northern Europeans looking for a Southern retreat.

I use the sale transaction history as a type of measurement similar to stocks where I look at the 52-week range of the stock trading range. Real estate is very much a Buy-and-Hold investment. The market will usually be more than what the city considers it to be worth. Read next section on "Understanding House Market Value vs. Assessed Value" on page 52.

Understanding House Market Value vs. Assessed Value

Market value is the most probable price as of a specific date (the date of sale) that a property with all its rights should sell after reasonable exposure to buyers in a competitive market with the sellers under no undue duress (meaning the sellers aren't forced to sell).

At its most basic form, house market value is usually the highest price that the home would bring on the real estate market if a reasonable length of time is allowed for the home to sell. In this scenario the buyer will have complete knowledge of the legal uses and purposes of the home.

Assessed value is the value of a property as of a certain date (usually January 1st) according to the tax rolls of your local government jurisdiction (county or city). This value can be higher or lower than market value based on the assessment ratio, which is a percentage of market value.

What is an Assessment ratio? The assessment ratio is the percentage that each state uses to determine the property taxes. A state will also determine whether you will be assessed per hundred or per thousand dollars. What does this mean?

Example – Your property's market value is $100,000 as of January 1st according to your county. Your neighborhood market activity is normally monitored by a county tax assessor over the course of one year. The assessment ratio in your state is 60%. You take $100,000 x 60% = $60,000. Now that $60,000 is your assessed value.

If you want to figure out the actual dollar amount in taxes you will pay, you take that $60,000 and divide it by 100 or 1,000 depending on your state (you can call your local jurisdiction and ask if your taxes are calculated per $100 or per $1,000). In this example your state assesses per 100. Take $60,000 / 100 = $600 x (your county tax rate) = the total amount in property taxes you pay per year!

Your county tax rate is usually set by your local elected officials. So, for example let us do a final calculation of the taxes of the above property with a tax rate of $1.23.

Final calculations:

$100,000 (market value) x 60% (assessment ratio) = $60,000 (assessed value) / 100 (state mill rate) = $600 x $1.23 (local county tax rate) = $738 in taxes you would pay your county for one year.

As you can see in this example, the county tax rate increased your taxes by 23% (23 cents over one dollar). You can also see how the county tax rate has nothing to do with the assessed value of your home. It was added after your assessed value was set. It's a way for government leaders to get more money to pay for county services and programs.

The property tax value (assessed value) of your home may not change unless certain circumstances occur, depending on the state and city where you live. Many states do not allow the assessment value to be increased unless the home is sold (California among others) or there are improvements done to the house. When you're looking at the assessed value versus market value of homes, in many cases you may notice that the house market value rises and falls, but the property tax value of the home usually stays stable and only changes if certain conditions occur.

Loan applications are part of the mortgage process, and the lender will compare the assessed value versus market value of the home. For the lender, the market value of the home is the more important of these two amounts, because this is the amount that the lender will use to value the home.

House market value can change frequently, and is dependent on the housing supply and demand as well as other factors, including the economy. The property tax value (assessed value) of a home can vary greatly given the factors above. Market value is the most accurate and stable as far as lenders are concerned. This value is preferred by lenders because it's based on facts and certain factors that reflect the true value of the home. This is the amount that is usually used for mortgage applications and home equity loans.

Property tax value (assessed value) is used more as a guide for lenders, but they know that value is set as of January 1st. So, if you're buying or building a home and it's July, that property tax value (assessed value) is seven months old. A bank will not lend money solely on a seven month old appraisal by your county. It's important to understand that there are some differences in the assessed value versus market value, and to know what these differences are.

Becoming a Landlord

You have a lot of resources available to you as a Landlord. I personally subscribe to the LPA (Landlord Protection Agency). This site gives you access to a network of other Landlords and provides monthly newsletters and articles to help you make the most of your new role as Landlord. It also provides forms for you such as Lease Agreements, Form Letters and much more. Here's a sample of some of the articles you'll find in the monthly newsletters which I find very informative:

- How to Screen Tenants in 5 easy steps   (http://www.thelpa.com/lpa/tips/5_step_screening.html)
- What do I do when the tenant doesn't pay   (http://www.thelpa.com/lpa/what/whattodo1.html)
- Tricks and Cons that Tenants use   (http://www.thelpa.com/lpa/what/tricks.html)
- Where's the Rent - Excuse of the Day   (http://www.thelpa.com/lpa/excuses.html)

By just reading the above article taglines you might be thinking that becoming a Landlord is for the brave of heart. However, that would be a misguided assumption. Being a Landlord can be a very rewarding business experience.

All you need as a Landlord is a sense responsibility to attend to matters that need your attention for the maintenance and upkeep of your investment. You are essentially running a business and elect custodians (tenants) based on their qualifications to look after your property. The nice part of running this business is that your custodians pay you for the privilege of living there. They pay the utility bills, look after your property and pay your mortgage / property taxes. Running a Bed-and-Breakfast operation is harder work than this. You are never obligated to make their bed or their breakfast.

You need to be fair. As a Landlord, you are always balancing the needs of the property with the needs of your tenants. It is not your responsibility to furnish them with luxury appliances or pool heaters or anything that would be considered above basic living conditions. You just need to provide an environment that is safe, clean and does not provide any danger to their health.

You always need to treat this as a business. You need to focus on top line income and bottom line profit. If you are losing money, that's not a successful business. Although you never want to become friends with your tenants, you want to make sure they are looked after in a courteous and professional way. If you neglect this facet of being a Landlord then your place doesn't look any better than the one down the street for the same price but may be closer to a shopping mall or to their place of work. Tenants do take into account their relationship with you as one consideration for where they choose to live. If they start looking elsewhere it will cost you in potentially lost rental income if your property stays empty.

Once you have this practiced, in terms of treating your tenants with respect and in a professional manner, you are on your way to becoming a host when you decide to convert your home into a Vacation Rental Property. It's basically a service business and the better you are at communicating with and helping people service their wants and needs, the better you will be at this business that will eventually come in the form of endorsements and referrals on your advertised property website. More is explained on this in the section entitled, Renting your Vacation Property on page 82.

As part of running a rental service business you will need forms. You can get a lot of free forms online at the LPA Free Forms (http://www.thelpa.com/lpa/free-forms.html) website. You can also get essential forms for the following areas:

- Leases, Addendums & Disclosures
  http://www.thelpa.com/lpa/forms.html#cat_1._leases,_addendums
- Rental Applications, Tenant Screening, Move-In
  http://www.thelpa.com/lpa/forms.html#cat_2._rental_applications
- Lease Enforcement and Rent Collection Forms

http://www.thelpa.com/lpa/forms.html#cat_3._lease_enforcement
- **Property Management Forms**
  http://www.thelpa.com/lpa/forms.html#cat_4._property_management

All these forms are available individually or as part of an annual membership. I'd recommend you get the 2 year membership ($57/year) which is only slightly more than the 1 Year membership for $89 but at least you'll get the Forms on a CD that will help you with any rental situation, and save you the effort of downloading each form from the internet. It also provides you with a monthly newsletter that continues even after your subscription expires. I don't get any fees for endorsing them. However, I do know that the value of the entire package over buying forms individually is a $575.00 value.

You should also sign up for the Quick Check Credit Report Service (http://thelpa.com/lpa/qc-signup.html) which can provide you with Tenant Credit History (http://www.thelpa.com/lpa/qc-sample_tu_credit_report.html), Criminal Background Check (http://www.thelpa.com/lpa/qc-sample-criminal-terrorist.html), Eviction Searches (http://www.thelpa.com/lpa/qc-sample-eviction.html), and Person Searches.

10 Steps to Finding the Right Tenant

In Florida, where your tenants can come from any part of the country, you need to be extra vigilant on their "story". I call it a "story" because that's usually what it sounds like when you interview them over the phone. You will hear their hardships and how the bank treated them unfairly or how their employer let them go after 25 years of dedicated service. This is very similar to a job interview where you look to qualifications to satisfy your needs. You are the interviewer and they are the applicant.

You will get a ton of inquiries and it helps if you know up front what kind of tenant you are looking for:

- Family with children (how many children, what ages)
- Pets (size and how many)
- Will you accept smokers (even if they smoke outside)
- Professional couple (no pets, no kids)
- Retired couple (no job, fixed income)

There's no right choice and each choice can come with complications or can be trouble free for years. I have found that using a multi-layered interview process which filters out candidates, works best for me. Let me share with you my 10 step process.

#	Process Step	See this section for further details
1.	Take good pictures of your property to attract potential tenants	"Prepare your Picture Library" – page 57
2.	Setup your Online Rental Inquiry Form	"Create your Online Rental Inquiry Form" – page 59
3.	Setup your Online Rental Application Form	"Your Online Rental Application Form" – Page 61
4.	Create a free website for your property – done in 1 hour	"Showcase your Property" – page 63
5.	Advertise your rental property for free	"How to Advertise your Listing" – page 65
6.	Call those applicants that look best qualified to you	"Tenant Interview and Screening Process" – page 70
7.	Schedule your property showings to qualified candidates	"Schedule your Property Showings" – page 71
8.	Get your deposit	"Get your Deposit" – page 72
9.	Do your background and credit checks	"Do your Background/Credit Checks" – page 73
10.	Get the lease signed	"Get the Lease Signed" – page 77

This 10 step process will get you setup so that your rental business becomes a well-oiled machine. If you plan to buy multiple properties, you need to perform the above. Even with only one property, this process will save you enormous amounts of time each time you search for new tenants, which happens to be the time intensive part of running a rental business. Also, this setup will help you when you are ready to rent out your property as a vacation rental because you will have your own website already and have the forms ready to go. Those tenants only stay for weeks or months, not years so the turnover will demand more of your time if you are not setup for an efficient operation. Besides, these are portable skills that I'm teaching you. I'm sure your creative genius will use these skills and methods in many other ways.

Prepare your Picture Library

Most rentals sell based on appearance. You want to accentuate the lifestyle that your tenants are attracted to. In Florida, pools are great assets and command higher rents.

If you are close to amenities, like shopping, drug store, restaurants, a Yachting Marina, fishing spots or Beaches, take pictures of those areas and post them also into your picture library.

Appliances like Fridge, Stove, Washer, Dryer, parking space and storage are key features for prospective tenants. Two other critical factors are location and cleanliness. These last two attributes will probably draw most of your potential calls. The size of the home can sometimes be a draw but as long as it's not small, you are probably safe and should aim at a home with at least 1800 square feet. Why 1800 square feet? I have found that most home sizes range between 1200-2000 square feet of living space – under air conditioning. That means 1600 would be the median size. Having something at 1800 will set your home apart from the average and be considered as one of the larger choices. Your pictures and description should emphasize these positives.

Try to get some pictures with the house when it has furniture in it. Even if the home was staged before you bought it, use some of those pictures. It gives a sense of how furniture could be laid out within your home giving it imaginable possibilities in the eyes of your prospects. I have found most people usually don't see the potential unless they are shown it. That's why fully furnished Model homes with all the upgrades help sell the home and stirs up the inspiration and motivation to buy.

Have at least one outside shot of the front for curb appeal. Even though it's a rental, your tenants will have friends and family come over for pool and barbeque parties. Even though they don't own the house, they still want to portray a sense of pride about where and how they live to their friends. It's just human nature at work.

I use Google's Picasa (http://picasaweb.google.com/home?hl=en&tab=wq) as my picture library. Here's why:

- It's free
- Allows you to store up to 1GB worth of photos. How many photos is that. That depends on your megapixels of your shots and you can use this calculator

  (http://web.forret.com/tools/megapixel.asp?width=2448&height=1632)
- to determine the number of photos. A 4.0 megapixel Camera can store 832 JPEG photos into a 1GB storage space (each photo would be 1.2 megabyte in size).
- Allows you to create Albums of Photos

- Allows you to create a Slideshow from an Album
- Allows you to Annotate or enter Captions that explain your photos as your slideshow plays
- Allows you to make Albums/Slideshows Publicly viewable
- Allows you to link directly to your Public Album from a Google website (see "Showcase your Property" - page 63)

Note: You will need to create a GMAIL Account and a PICASA Google Account, it's free and it's instant. It will also be useful for the next step when you use Google Documents to create your online inquiry and application forms (described in section "Create your Online Rental Inquiry Form" on page 59).

Create your Online Rental Inquiry Form

Now that you have a GMAIL Account and a Google Account from the previous step when you created a Picture Library using Picasa, you are ready for the next step in creating an online rental inquiry form.

Online forms are created using Google spreadsheets. Google spreadsheets are very similar to Microsoft Excel spreadsheets. Spreadsheets are nothing more than rows and columns of information in a table format that looks like a grid. You start by created a spreadsheet in Google Documents. When prompted sign in with your Google GMAIL Account.

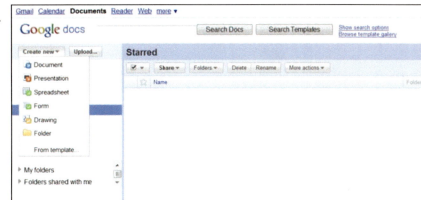

On the upper left is a [▼] button.

Click on it and select the **Form** dropdown choice. Forms are special types of spreadsheets.

For example, let's say you want to collect the following information about people that saw your advertisement for a rental property.

- First Name
- Last Name
- Email Address
- Phone Number
- Comment or Questions
- Do you have Pets?
- # of Adults
- # of Children
- Lease Term
- # of Smokers

As your form comes up, create your first question title. This could be simply **First Name** if you want. Keep the Question type as **Text** and check the selection to **Make this a required question**. When finished click **Done**.

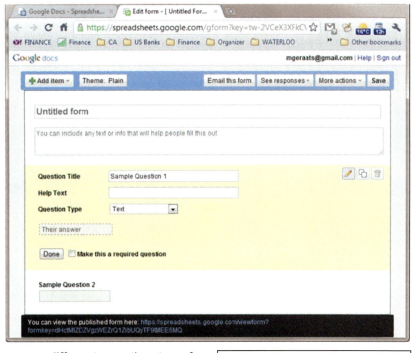

The form will collapse the first question area and allow you see what it looks like. The red asterisk * next to the question means it is a required entry field.

To edit the **Sample Question 2**, you simply press the Pencil Icon to edit that selection. Keep doing this until you have all the above fields. You may want to choose a different question type for things that specify quantities, like # of Adults, # of Children, Lease Term and # of Smokers. You do this by choosing Multiple Choice, instead of Text.

This saves the person filling in the form from typing. All they need to do is select a radio button.

Lease Term *
Preferred Lease (in years)
○ 1 Year
○ 2 Years
○ 3 Years

When you are through creating your form fields, click on **Untitled Form** section at the top and give your form a name. Call it **Rental Inquiry** *<address of your property>*.

Click **Save** on the upper right of the form. Next click on the **More Actions** button next to the **Save** button you just pressed and select **Edit Confirmation**. Here you can edit your response to say "Thank you for your submission. Your inquiry has been submitted to the property owner for consideration."

To test out your new form, click on the link at the bottom of the form in the Black Ribbon area where it says: **You can view the published form here**

Enter in some test data and then click on **Go Back to the Form**. Now click your Google Documents library by clicking the link in the form below that says Powered by Google Docs.

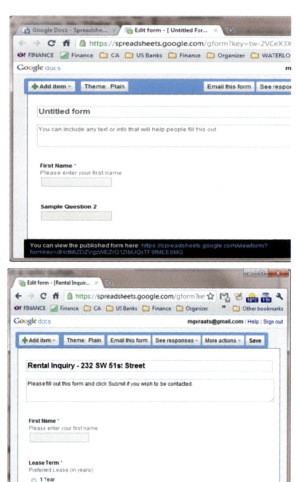

This form will now show up in your Google Documents library. Have a look at the entries, which are automatically date and time stamped.

Now you have a spreadsheet that will collect responses from potential renters by entering in information through a Web Published Inquiry Form.

But how will you know when they entered in information?

Easy, get Google to notify you immediately via email when the form (or spreadsheet rather) gets new information. You can do this by selecting the **Tools** dropdown menu from within your spreadsheet and selecting **Notification Rules**.

Select how you want to be notified (options shown below).

Now you have pretty much everything setup to start polling for inquiries, gaining a Contact Form so you can call back those that meet your criteria for the ideal tenant.

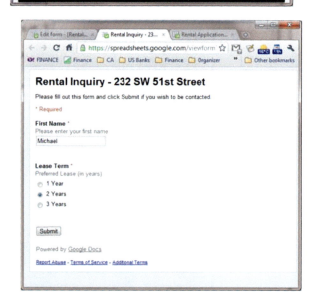

Your Online Rental Application Form

Now that you have the skill at creating online forms that can capture and store information from potential tenants, you should create yourself an application form as well. This form has all the same questions to collect information about your tenants that the paper copy form has from the LPA (Landlord Protection Association - Becoming a Landlord on page 54).

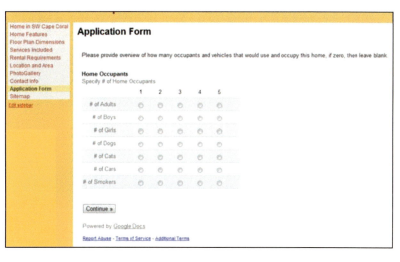

The problem with hard copy forms are the logistics/exchange of information gets complicated. You email or fax the form to them. They fill in the forms with their own hand-writing, which is sometimes hard to read or they leave fields blank where you need information on. They fax it back to you, or scan it and email it back. A fax or scan can result in lost clarity or sharpness which just adds to readability problems.

An online form:

- captures the information for you;
- date and time stamps it;
- performs field entry validation for you – some fields are required;
- ensures all fields will be legible (like a Social Security Number);
- logs it in a spreadsheet (Google cloud) and accessible from anywhere;
- and notifies you by email with a link to it when it's ready for viewing;

What could be easier than that? It will save you enormous amounts of time and frustration.

As you can see from the first image on this page, I capture some context about the applicant. It helps knowing what their family profile looks like and whether it matches your search criteria.

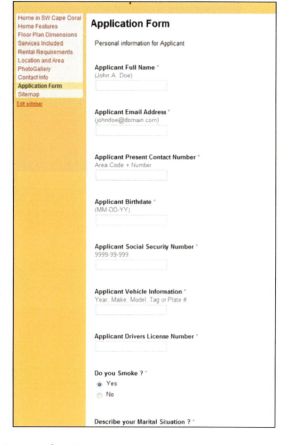

This form is another important piece as it pulls together your property profile. The way you do this is by creating a Website for your property using Google Sites. Google Sites can link directly to your Google Docs Form. Google Sites can also link directly to Google's Picasa where you have your pictures stored for your property. You can also provide location information to your audience using Google Maps. By now, you probably see a theme. Google has a lot of integration amongst its own tools and I use this to my advantage.

Best of all, you haven't spent a single dime, because it's all free.

The only investment you've made is time. However, this investment will pay back for you in spades, many times over.

As I mentioned before, once you learn these tricks, you'll apply them to many other situations in your life. Perhaps you want to keep track of your stock portfolio, or coordinate a family reunion and are requesting family members to register or RSVP at your website using forms. You are only limited by your imagination.

Showcase your Property

You might be asking yourself at this point, why I'm going through all this trouble to just rent out a place. Is it overkill?

It is elaborate but I'm preparing you for something much larger and more lucrative down the road. Since my plan is to market my property as a vacation rental, these websites, forms and tools will come in very handy.

If you are receiving calls or inquiries about a rental place where the tenant plans to stay for 1-2 years, think of the turnover required for someone who's only interested in staying for a month or just 2 weeks. Although you may decide to hand over your property to a vacation rental agency, which is fine, you can make more money by not having to share your vacation property income with someone else. They typically retain 20% or more of your income for listing it, accepting payment, coordinating entry and scheduling cleanup after the vacationers leave. At first, you could use them, but eventually you want to list on your own, if you are looking to retain more income.

This isn't rocket science and taking a stepped approach is quite acceptable.

Besides, if you showcase your property as though it was a vacation retreat, you are going to attract more potential tenants towards your home and away from the competing landlords in the area.

Take time to explain the **Location and Area** with lots of enticing pictures. Your tenants will most likely come from out of

---

Home in SW Cape Coral
Home Features
Floor Plan Dimensions
Services Included
Rental Requirements
Location and Area
PhotoGallery
Contact Info
Application Form
Sitemap

Edit sidebar

Location and Area

Go shopping nearby at the Promenade in Cape Harbor and check out the boutiques for some great values. After all that shopping your feet will guide you towards RumRunners Restaurant to sit and watch the Yachts go by. There's a band playing almost every weekend as you enjoy fabulous sunsets. There's also numerous bike paths along Eldorado Parkway as it winds up Surfside Blvd to the multi-million dollar homes on the water. Also remember that you are never more than 20 minutes away from Fort Myers Beach across the Cape Coral Bridge or Sanibel and Captiva. Try **Snug Harbor** for dinner in Fort Myers Beach or go the **Ellingtons** for Jazz, Dinner and Dancing on Sanibel Island.

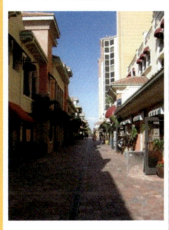

Home in SW Cape Coral
Home Features
Floor Plan Dimensions
Services Included
Rental Requirements
Location and Area
PhotoGallery
Contact Info
Application Form
Sitemap

Edit sidebar

Home Features

Address:

- 5337 SW 21st Pl Cape Coral FL 33914
- Comes unfurnished, pictures on main page are from 2009
- Color schemes on walls are Taupe and Camel (as shown on home page)

Features:

- Landlord is Financially stable - no risk of Foreclosure or Short Sale
- Year Built in 2000
- Lot Size = 9,931 sq ft / 0.23 acres (80 feet wide by 125 feet deep)
- 1542 Square Feet of living space under Central Air
- 3 Bedrooms and 2 full Bathrooms
- 2 Car Garage (437 Square feet) - attached with automatic garage door opener
- Automatic Lawn Irrigation System from Well water
- Split Floor Plan
- Open Concept with Kitchen overlooking Living room and outdoor pool and Lanai
- Pool facing South East with 15' tall hedges for complete privacy
- 20" Tile throughout entire home
- High Efficiency Front Load Washer with High Spin Cycle and HE Dryer for lower utility bills

Recent Upgrades:

- 2009 - New Air Conditioner 3.5 Ton 13 Seer installed
- 2009 - New ducting installed throughout entire house to each bedroom
- 2009 - New Pool light installed for night time enjoyment of pool
- 2009 - New Low flush Efficiency toilet installed in Master Ensuite bathroom
- 2009 - Home tiled throughout with 20" porcelain tile for

5337 SW 21st Pl

---

state as I've found in most cases. They usually get job relocations, or decide they had enough of the cold weather during the winter months and would like to work in a tropical climate.

Another section of your website should describe the **Home Features**. Describe the upgrades you made recently. Describe the appliances and whether they are new or their water and electricity saving features, since that will save them on monthly utility bills.

Also add a Section called **Rental Requirements**. This will explain the Move-In Requirements you are looking for in terms of First Month rent plus Security Deposit. In Canada we call it "First and Last". However, that's not as smart as holding a Security Deposit. They still pay you last month's rent. You return the Security Deposit after inspecting on move-out day.

How to Advertise your Listing

There's really one answer to this and that's anything that's free for tenants to see what's available. They won't buy a newspaper or magazine to find available rentals. That means it's most likely going to be http://www.craigslist.org.

Therefore as a home owner, you want to list your property in the Housing section. If you are renting a property in Sarasota then you need the locale specific Craigslist. The Web address you put into your browser will usually have the city as the first part of the Web address. For Sarasota it would be http://Sarasota.craigslist.org and for SW Florida it would be http://fortmyers.craigslist.org.

This of course is another free service for you as the Landlord. However, before you go creating a listing, search for properties with similar features and in the same location as yours. This will give you an idea of how much you can ask for in rent.

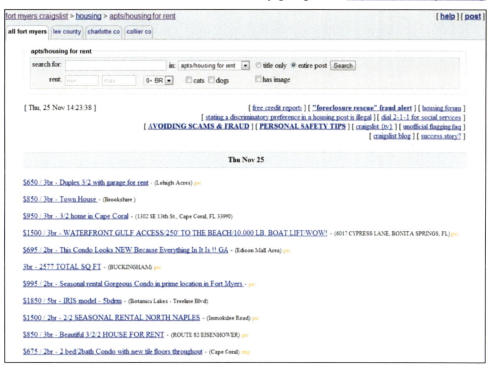

Your add will go up within 15 minutes and will be active for 30 days, but it does move down in the list that seems to grow by about 100 entries per day. So your advertisement will be less visible as days go by. However, don't worry, savvy Craigslist renters search on keywords and by location and within price ranges. Therefore, your property will show in the narrowed search results if you have a comparable property to other listings. That's why I said to go look first so that your demands are within reason. Pool homes on average will fetch an average $100 more per month.

Tour Ad Title is your eye catcher. Spend some time thinking of your property's most attractive feature and use that in your Ad Title somehow. Pictures can sell a property. It can also deter people if your pictures choices are poor with low lighting or out of focus conditions. Just remember to take pictures with full sunlight outside, or clear blue sky. Accentuate the positives. You are limited to posting up to 4 pictures.

Looking at the screen snapshot above you'll see many people don't spend a lot of time on this and others are clearly motivated. Compare the two entries above:

$850 / 3br – Town House – (Brookshire)

$1500 / 3br WATERFRONT GULF ACCESS / 250' TO THE BEACH / 10,000 BOAT LIFT / WOW! – (6017 Cypress Lane) pic

Of course one is double the price of the other for the same number of bedrooms, but if the first person used some more enthusiasm in his ad, for half the price, it would create more demand, especially since his ad didn't have any pictures.

However, I believe that even the 2nd Advertisement could be made much more appealing. Let's look at an example. The next page has this person's advertisement for the WATERFRONT GULF ACCESS. I'm going to change it on the following page to let you see the BEFORE and AFTER and how I would write it.

Remember that Craigslist will remove your advertisement if it attempts to look for a specific type of Renter, like saying, "This property would be ideal for a Professional Couple without Kids or Pets". Your intention might be innocent because of the size of property but it will appear as blocking equal access to everyone from applying. What you ultimately decide to accept as your ideal tenant is your decision. However, Craigslist will prevent you from seeking out specific communities or profiles of people for your property and will remove your advertisement if they determine it to have discriminatory content within it. This protects you from being sued and that's a good thing.

$1500 / 3br WATERFRONT GULF ACCESS / 250' TO THE BEACH / 10,000 BOAT LIFT / WOW!

THIS HOME IS A BOATERS-FISHERMANS-BEACH WALKERS DREAM. LESS THAN 250' TO THE WAVES/BEACH. 10,000 LB. BOAT LIFT. ON 50' OF SEAWALL, 5 MINUTES TO THE GULF. GARAGE UNDER AIR, 2 EXTRA DOUBLEWIDE DRIVEWAYS, TO ACCOMMODATE 4 VEHICLES, BOAT TRAILERS AND/OR BOATS. NEWER PVC VINYL FENCED AREA FOR PETS, ETC. LARGE CORNER LOT ON A GOOD CANAL, EXTRA STORAGE BLDG. HEAVY METAL BAHAMA STORM SHUTTERS, LANDSCAPPING PROVIDES PRIVACY. LANAI. LOW MAINTENANCE YARD. OUTDOOR SHOWER, AUTOMATIC GARAGE DOOR OPENER, GRAND WOOD INTERIOR BLINDS (WINDOW COVERINGS) THROUGHOUT, ITALIAN PORCELAN TILE FLOORS THROUGHOUT, WAINSCOT THROUGHOUT, EAT-IN KITCHEN WITH PANTRY, GE PROFILE STAINLESS STEEL APPLIANCES. NEW A/C AND WATER HEATER. LOT SIZE: 50 x 125 x 50 x 125 (CORNER LOT) . LIVING AREA: 1272. TOTAL AREA: 1686. HOME IS UNFURNISHED. VERY NICE NEIGHBORHOOD!

LIVE THE GOOD LIFE...BEACH, GULF OF MEXICO, ESTERO BAY.......YOU WON'T FIND A BETTER "VALUE" ANYWHERE !!!

CALL GINA @ (239)495-7459

PLEASE NOTE:*****PROPERTY AVAILABLE ON JANUARY 1, 2011*******

cats are OK - purrr
dogs are OK - wooof
Location: 6017 CYPRESS LANE, BONITA SPRINGS, FL

[$1495 / 3br Boater's Dream – Minutes to Beach – Available Jan 1, 2011](#)

This home has it all for that Boat or Beach Lover

Welcome to 6017 CYPRESS LANE, BONITA SPRINGS, FL

Features:

- Stainless Steel Appliances (GE Profile)
- Eat-in Kitchen with Pantry
- New A/C and Water Heater
- Porcelain Tile Floors Throughout
- Low Maintenance Yard with Fencing for your Pets or young children
- Storm Shutters (Bahama - Heavy Metal)
- 1272 sq. ft. living area (under air) – 1686 sq. ft. total
- 10,000 LB Boat Lift
- Less than 250 Feet to Beach - Less than 5 minutes Sailing to Gulf
- Oversize Garage All under Air
- Double driveways for up to 4 Cars/Trailers/Boats
- Outdoor Shower

Submit your interest by filling in our contact form at https://sites.google.com/site/6017cypresslanebonitasprings/contact-info

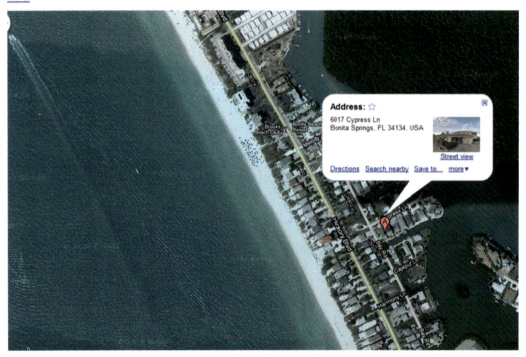

See the difference? Here's what I changed:

- No longer used CAPS all over the place and no need to accentuate with excessive exclamation marks or asterisks, (this isn't Vegas baby);
- Used Bullets for the key points – make for an easier read and keeps them going down the list in the order you want;
- Changed the Title to target a specific type of tenant. Also put when Available if it isn't immediately next month as most tenants searching already have given notice and must move out. This is important planning information for them;
- Put an Address for them so they can see the same picture above when they use the Google Maps link in the ad, Craigslist creates one for you if you provide the exact address in the field;

- OK, I reduced the price by $5, but it puts us in a different camp;
- Used only 1 picture instead of 4. I mean, look at the gleaming water, the beach? Doesn't this one sell itself?
- I placed the things that the woman of the house will like the most near the top of the list, Stainless Steel appliances, pantry, Eat-in Kitchen, porcelain tile floors throughout, for easier cleaning. Storm Shutters for safety. Fenced Yard for containing small kids and pets to play with.
- No more direct phone number. You'll get all kinds of cranks calling you. Give them a link to your Contact Form you created earlier (see "Create your Online Rental Inquiry Form" on page 59), then you call them.

Tenant Interview and Screening Process

Once you start getting inquiries from potential tenants, here's a chart to help you navigate your search for the ideal tenant.

It's not foolproof and you need to use common sense, your instinct and your judge of character as a guide. However, this method at least might but some objectivity into your search, and gives you a way to score your tenants through your interview process. The best source of information for "Becoming a Landlord" is detailed on page 54.

It's not necessary to meet your tenants in person. I sometimes meet my tenant months after accepting them into the property and after they've lived there for a while. External appearances may sometimes disguise a great tenant or a poor one. The two usually don't always correlate with each other. Their rental history, references, and job situation is usually the more important elements to consider when you look for credible and trustworthy tenants for your property. Remember, you cannot discriminate on race, religion, sex as this is an illegal offence. Besides, it has no bearing to a good/bad tenant.

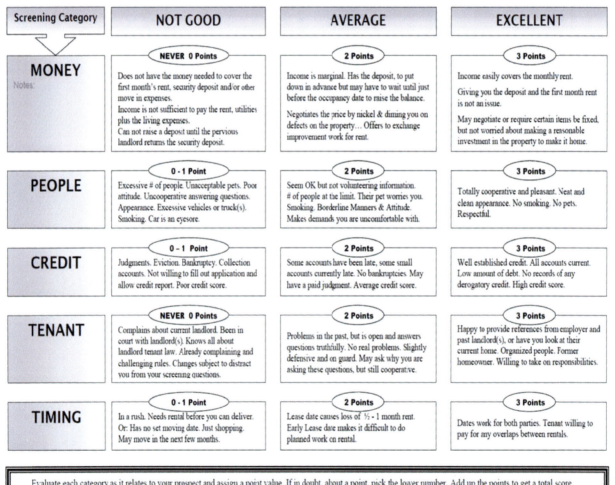

Screening Category	NOT GOOD	AVERAGE	EXCELLENT
MONEY Notes:	**NEVER 0 Points** Does not have the money needed to cover the first month's rent, security deposit and/or other move in expenses. Income is not sufficient to pay the rent, utilities plus the living expenses. Can not raise a deposit until the pervious landlord returns the security deposit.	**2 Points** Income is marginal. Has the deposit, to put down in advance but may have to wait until just before the occupancy date to raise the balance. Negotiates the price by nickel & diming you on defects on the property... Offers to exchange improvement work for rent.	**3 Points** Income easily covers the monthly rent. Giving you the deposit and the first month rent is not an issue. May negotiate or require certain items be fixed, but not worried about making a reasonable investment in the property to make it home.
PEOPLE	**0 - 1 Point** Excessive # of people. Unacceptable pets. Poor attitude. Uncooperative answering questions. Appearance. Excessive vehicles or truck(s). Smoking. Car is an eyesore.	**2 Points** Seem OK but not volunteering information. # of people at the limit. Their pet worries you. Smoking. Borderline Manners & Attitude. Makes demands you are uncomfortable with.	**3 Points** Totally cooperative and pleasant. Neat and clean appearance. No smoking. No pets. Respectful.
CREDIT	**0 - 1 Point** Judgments. Eviction. Bankruptcy. Collection accounts. Not willing to fill out application and allow credit report. Poor credit score.	**2 Points** Some accounts have been late, some small accounts currently late. No bankruptcies. May have a paid judgment. Average credit score.	**3 Points** Well established credit. All accounts current. Low amount of debt. No records of any derogatory credit. High credit score.
TENANT	**NEVER 0 Points** Complains about current landlord. Been in court with landlord(s). Knows all about landlord tenant law. Already complaining and challenging rules. Changes subject to distract you from your screening questions.	**2 Points** Problems in the past, but is open and answers questions truthfully. No real problems. Slightly defensive and on guard. May ask why you are asking these questions, but still cooperative.	**3 Points** Happy to provide references from employer and past landlord(s), or have you look at their current home. Organized people. Former homeowner. Willing to take on responsibilities.
TIMING	**0 - 1 Point** In a rush. Needs rental before you can deliver. Or: Has no set moving date. Just shopping. May move in the next few months.	**2 Points** Lease date causes loss of ½ - 1 month rent. Early Lease date makes it difficult to do planned work on rental.	**3 Points** Dates work for both parties. Tenant willing to pay for any overlaps between rentals.

Evaluate each category as it relates to your prospect and assign a point value. If in doubt, about a point, pick the lower number. Add up the points to get a total score.

- Any score below 9 is not acceptable.
- Prospects scoring in the range of 9 – 11 are the tenants that can occupy most of your property management time.
- The most successful landlords always rent to prospects in the 12 – 15 range.

TOTAL SCORE:

Schedule your Property Showings

Now that you advertised your property in Craigslist (How to Advertise your Listing – page 65) and directed people to your website (Showcase your Property- page 63) to fill in a Contact Inquiry form (Create your Online Rental Inquiry Form – page 59), you have narrowed down your list to the ideal candidates and called them to perform a quick interview by phone (Tenant Interview and Screening Process – page 70).

You have created a shortlist of interested tenants that you feel as qualified. Now they actually want to see the property to see if they like it on the inside. For every 10 people that contact you about your property, you'll probably have 3 that make it to this round where you feel they may be an ideal tenant. Now you need to let them in to see your place to see if they want to actually live there.

You'll need to hire someone to allow them in. I have a really good real estate agent that lives in the area that can provide access to the property. Although she does this for me as a favour because we have bought several homes through her and because she has a heart of gold - I compensate her with a financial bonus after I get it rented.

I'm not present to meet those people. My agent provides feedback to me on the people coming to see the property. This helps me get her perspective, as a local person, on the character attributes of the people coming to see the place. She will also tell me how excited or not they seemed about moving forward to the next step, which is to contact me to provide a Security Deposit to hold this place for them.

Sometimes it works well when you schedule other interested parties to come at about the same time. It saves my agent from making multiple trips but it also creates an open house effect where these interested parties see that others have an interest in this place too. It tells them that if they are really interested, they need to move quickly with their Security Deposit.

Having a real estate agent show the property instead of the landlord has worked out well for me. Agents are experienced with people and experienced with showing home features and can provide comment on the neighborhood, schools, shopping areas and amenities. The landlord has a different relationship and it's best to keep physical appearances out of the decision process to this point because it allows you to make an objective decision versus subjective.

Follow-up with those that expressed interest in your property. My agent tells me who she felt really liked the property. I call them immediately, while the experience and feeling about the property is fresh in their minds. If they tell me that they really liked it then I ask them to secure the listing with a Security Deposit explained in the next section.

Get your Deposit

A Security Deposit is a serious commitment of interest in your property. It is a financial commitment that is usually equal to one month rent. It is also a non-refundable if they back out of the deal. It allows you to process their application form (Your Online Rental Application Form – page 61) which they fill in with specific references and social security numbers and driver's license numbers for you to use as part of your background and credit check.

I advertised my property this past year and on 3 separate occasions after showing the property where the people wanted to move-in, turn around and backed out of the deal. The first couple had no kids, no pets and the husband had just lost his job. They provided a Security Deposit, which I could have kept, but considering their situation, I returned it to them. The last thing they needed after losing income from work was one month rent for a property they'll never move-in to.

The second situation was a lady that was separated from her husband, was going to sell her huge home, because she could no longer afford the mortgage on her own, then turned around and told me that she worked out the situation with her bank. This happened after I kept asking for her Security Deposit but did not get returned emails until I finally reached her by phone.

The third situation, as I was getting within 2 weeks from when my current tenant was going to move out, was a lady that transferred jobs from Ohio to Florida and worked for a large grocery chain. She was an HR Manager and actually came down for her first meeting. The job market was so fragile that the company retracted the offer to re-locate her. I wasn't given all the details, but this time, I kept the Security Deposit to cover my loss of income should my tenant move-out and I had no new tenant to move in. I was lucky, I found someone that really loved the place and they moved down from Sarasota within 2 weeks.

The Security Deposit is an important step for you as the landlord and it is part of closing the deal with the people that are most qualified and most interested in your property.

The Security Deposit should be held while you process their application form. The Security Deposit needs to be returned to them if you decide not to move forward based on the results of their Rental Application submission. You need to state the reason for not accepting them, such as based on credit history, previous references etc. Details are not necessary, just the area of concern that helped you make your decision.

Once you accept your new tenants and give them approval of their rental application, you then use the Security Deposit as your retainer to cover any **Settlement Charges** to cover repairs when they move out.

Supply your new tenants in advance with these charges to ensure they are aware of the costs. This will help them focus on keeping it clean, free of repair and will ensure a smooth transition process to your new tenants.

Your tenants will be motivated to ensure they receive their Security Deposit back from you in full when they move out. In fact, they'll need this as their Security Deposit for the next place.

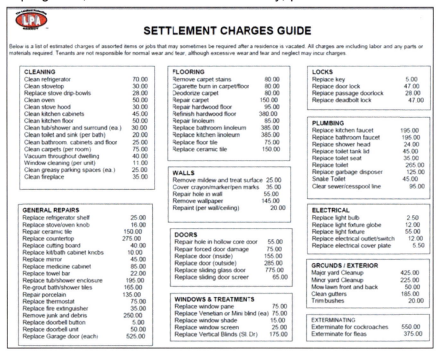

SETTLEMENT CHARGES GUIDE

Below is a list of estimated charges of assorted items or jobs that may sometimes be required after a residence is vacated. All charges are including labor and any parts or materials required. Tenants are not responsible for normal wear and tear, although excessive wear and tear and neglect may incur charges.

CLEANING

Clean refrigerator	70.00
Clean stovetop	30.00
Replace stove drip-bowls	28.00
Clean oven	50.00
Clean stove hood	30.00
Clean kitchen cabinets	45.00
Clean kitchen floor	50.00
Clean tub/shower and surround (ea.)	30.00
Clean toilet and sink (per bath)	20.00
Clean bathroom. cabinets and floor	25.00
Clean carpets (per room)	75.00
Vacuum throughout dwelling	40.00
Window cleaning (per unit)	11.00
Clean greasy parking spaces (ea.)	25.00
Clean fireplace	35.00

GENERAL REPAIRS

Replace refrigerator shelf	25.00
Replace stove/oven knob	16.00
Repair ceramic tile	150.00
Replace countertop	275.00
Replace cutting board	40.00
Replace kit/bath cabinet knobs	10.00
Replace mirror	45.00
Replace medicine cabinet	85.00
Replace towel bar	22.00
Replace tub/shower enclosure	195.00
Re-grout bath/shower tiles	165.00
Repair porcelain	135.00
Replace thermostat	75.00
Replace fire extinguisher	35.00
Remove junk and debris	250.00
Replace doorbell button	5.00
Replace doorbell unit	50.00
Replace Garage door (each)	525.00

FLOORING

Remove carpet stains	80.00
Cigarette burn in carpet/floor	80.00
Deodorize carpet	80.00
Repair carpet	150.00
Repair hardwood floor	95.00
Refinish hardwood floor	380.00
Repair linoleum	85.00
Replace bathroom linoleum	385.00
Replace kitchen linoleum	385.00
Replace floor tile	75.00
Replace ceramic tile	150.00

WALLS

Remove mildew and treat surface	25.00
Cover crayon/marker/pen marks	35.00
Repair hole in wall	55.00
Remove wallpaper	145.00
Repaint (per wall/ceiling)	20.00

DOORS

Repair hole in hollow core door	55.00
Repair forced door damage	75.00
Replace door (inside)	155.00
Replace door (outside)	285.00
Replace sliding glass door	775.00
Replace sliding door screen	65.00

WINDOWS & TREATMENTS

Replace window pane	75.00
Replace Venetian or Mini blind (ea)	75.00
Replace window shade	15.00
Replace window screen	25.00
Replace Vertical Blinds (Sl. Dr)	175.00

LOCKS

Replace key	5.00
Replace door lock	47.00
Replace passage doorlock	28.00
Replace deadbolt lock	47.00

PLUMBING

Replace kitchen faucet	195.00
Replace bathroom faucet	195.00
Replace shower head	24.00
Replace toilet tank lid	45.00
Replace toilet seat	35.00
Replace toilet	265.00
Replace garbage disposer	125.00
Snake Toilet	45.00
Clear sewer/cesspool line	95.00

ELECTRICAL

Replace light bulb	2.50
Replace light fixture globe	12.00
Replace light fixture	55.00
Replace electrical outlet/switch	12.00
Replace electrical cover plate	5.50

GROUNDS / EXTERIOR

Major yard Cleanup	425.00
Minor yard Cleanup	225.00
Mow lawn front and back	50.00
Clean gutters	185.00
Trim bushes	20.00

EXTERMINATING

Exterminate for cockroaches	550.00
Exterminate for fleas	375.00

Having them know in advance will make sure they treat your place like it's their own.

Do your Background/Credit Checks

As mentioned in a previous section Becoming a Landlord (page 50) performing credit and background checks are part of processing your application.

You should perform this check on each Adult that will live in your property. I charge a service fee that covers the costs for doing this and is due along with submitting the Security Deposit. Part of your Rental Application needs to get permission to perform this credit and background check. It covers you in case you were ever challenged by any authorities on accessing this information without consent as part of FCRA (Fair Credit Report Act). I have it as a check box on my online rental application and tell them the fee for this check. These fees are non-refundable even if you don't accept the tenants based on your findings.

You should also sign up for:

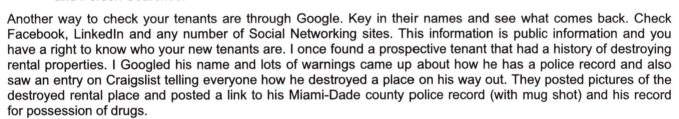

- Quick Check Credit Report Service

- Tenant Credit History

- Criminal Background Check

- Eviction Searches

- and Person Searches.

Another way to check your tenants are through Google. Key in their names and see what comes back. Check Facebook, LinkedIn and any number of Social Networking sites. This information is public information and you have a right to know who your new tenants are. I once found a prospective tenant that had a history of destroying rental properties. I Googled his name and lots of warnings came up about how he has a police record and also saw an entry on Craigslist telling everyone how he destroyed a place on his way out. They posted pictures of the destroyed rental place and posted a link to his Miami-Dade county police record (with mug shot) and his record for possession of drugs.

Also make sure you visit The National Tenant Reporting Company or ScreeningWorks which contain no fly lists for prospective tenants. It provides information on such things as:

- **Late payments**
- **Non-payment of rent**
- **Destruction of property**
- **Theft**
- **Refusal to vacate premises**
- **Or, any other issues a landlord may have encountered**

If you are already a member of the LPA (Landlord Protection Agency) you can gain access to the Deadbeat Tenant database through the NTRB (National Tenant Rating Bureau)

It is estimated that 95% of all tenant problems can be avoided through proper screening process.

Did you ever think the landlord reference the tenant gives you on your rental application might be false? Unfortunately, it is very common for a rental applicant to offer up a fake landlord reference, especially when he does not want you to hear what that landlord has to say about him. The purpose of The Landlord Reference Qualifier is to help you to determine if the information being given to you by the tenants' current or past landlord is the truth.

This screening technique has been successfully tested over time by professional landlords. By asking certain targeted questions, you will be able to spot a false reference much easier. An imposter most likely will not be able to answer anything more than the most basic and obvious questions that he or she may have been briefed on.

There's a sample form on the next page you can use, but I recommend you join the LPA for a complete list of very useful Forms.

I have never had a bad tenant so far. I make use of all the resources available to me and fortunately I've been protected.

LANDLORD REFERENCE QUALIFIER

The purpose of this form is to help you qualify the *reference* of a tenant. As we know, rental applicants sometimes furnish us with false information in order to circumvent the screening process. Below are suggested questions and topics to touch on when conducting your interview with a current or past landlord. Have your completed Rental Application on hand to cross-verify the information the tenant has given. But first, a little bit of advice: Remember to ask your questions in a way that the subject is required to provide you with information.

1. Mr. and Mrs. *Tenant* listed you as a reference on their application to rent from us.
    How did you come to know them?   *(Allow the subject to state that he or she is the landlord)*

_____

2. How long have they been tenants of yours?
_____

3. Let me just verify the address they are coming from. Could you please tell me the address they're moving from?

_____
    (This is important that the landlord knows the address of where his tenants are moving from.)

4. Would you mind just verifying the rent amount they've been paying? $_____
    (See if it matches the information on your application.)

5. What was the reason they decided to move?   _____

6. Is there any reason your name didn't come up on the tax records as the owner?
    (Ask this only if you searched the tax records and his name didn't come up!)
    _____

8. How old is the house (or building)?_____

9. How long have you owned it? _____

10. How many bedrooms did your place have? _____

11. Do these tenants smoke?   _____

12. Do these tenants have any pets?   _____ What kind? _____ How many?_____

13. Do you have a lease with these people? _____ If so, How long was the lease for? _____

14. By what method do they pay the rent?   With cash?   Do they mail a check?   Any bounced checks?

15. Would you say they were late with the rent in the last year more than 5 times or less than 5?

16. Can you tell me about any lease violations or disagreements - even small ones?
_____

17. What condition do they /did they keep (or leave) your rental in? _____

18. On a scale of 1 to 10, with 10 being the best, how would you rate these tenants?   _____

A few tips:

- You don't need to use all these questions. You may think of some to add on.
- Sometimes you may want to provide an incorrect address to the subject to see if he corrects you.
- Try to conduct this as respectfully and politely as possible. Explain that you are very careful about who you rent to. Tell him you appreciate the time you are being given.
- The idea of this is to find out if this is a legitimate landlord reference and to gain information about the tenants. Try to notice any inconsistencies with the tenants and landlord's stories.

Get the Lease Signed

When you get this far, after approving the rental application, getting the Security Deposit and Screening Fees, you are ready to get the Lease Signed. You should avoid going month to month and should always have a plan to lease on an annual basis. That way, as Landlord, you are getting 60 days' notice if your tenant notifies you on their intent to vacate, which gives you 60 days to find a new tenant. Going month to month, they only need to notify you in writing 30 days in advance on their intention to move-out.

Your lease is your written contract and is the final stage in ensuring both you and your tenants can see eye to eye on how to carry forward in this new relationship. If there are disagreements on the lease terms then you need to work them out or notify each other that you cannot come to terms and must look for someone who can comply with your terms.

Some of the terms I've had trouble with in the past is number of days you are willing to accept late rent payments. In Florida the number of days is 3 and is referred to as Pay Rent or Quit Notice. My lease states that for every day they are late paying rent, over and above the agreed to rent payment day (1st of the month), they will be charged $10/day on top of the monthly rent – not to exceed 15 days or they risk default. So far it has worked in keeping my rent payments on time.

Your lease should also specify responsibilities like mowing the lawn, or cleaning the pool and should specify regular maintenance or cleaning activities you expect them to perform, such as replacing the pool filter every 12 months with a new one. Remember that tenants will try to find the lowest level of commitment they need to perform. It's your responsibility to set the boundaries and the lease is where it should be specified in writing.

Once you have the lease signed, you have commitment. Next, you need to send your tenants some additional forms. All these forms are roughly the rules of engagement so that they understand there responsibility and consequences if the rules are not followed. Some forms you should be sending them are as follows:

- Appliance Agreement
- Pet Agreement – with Pet Deposit
- No Smoking Notice Reminder
- Periodic Inspection Report
- Property Condition Report
- Satellite Dish and Cable TV Addendum

These are some of the forms you may want to use to specify that this is an ongoing business relationship and that you will be actively involved in supporting your tenants but also making sure they hold up their end of the duty to look after your place.

If you don't hear from your tenants on a regular basis, then you need to contact them to check on how things are going. My experience has shown that tenants that don't stay in touch such as reporting minor property repairs usually tend to be problematic tenants. You need to reach out to them to find out what's going on, especially if you don't live in the area.

Make a list of what they report to you during your conversation and act upon having those things fixed. That doesn't mean you need to fix them all. The tenant is responsible for minor repairs under $100. If you act on the other repairs, your tenant will feel obligated to hold up their part.

Call them back to follow-up on it. If after calling back several times and you don't get resolution then serve them with a Lease Violation Notice which tells them that they are not complying with the lease terms. Mention in the letter the dates you discussed this matter with them and give them a due date to comply.

If you can, try to make the lease dates starting August 1. This is when lots of people need a rental if they are relocating since most people especially with kids will use the summer months to move as they don't have to pull their kids out of school. It is also a time where they need to get their kids signed up and approved for the new school. In order to do this, they will need a rental agreement to show that live in the neighborhood. Schools start in the third week of August in Florida, before our Labor day.

Rental Business Operations

Now that you have tenants and someone to look after your place, you can switch into cruise control. I call it cruise control because getting your tenant is like a pilot preparing for a flight, doing all the necessary pre-flight checks, following procedure checklists then taking off.

Now that you are airborne you just need to keep that airplane in the air flying straight without doing anything radical but also keeping an eye on things as you go, never getting complacent or falling asleep at the controls. The only time you need to worry about landing is when your tenant notifies you with intent to move-out. That means you need to start preparing for landing configuration and procedures. Shortly after landing you will start on performing all of the above steps again as you prepare for another take off. Ask any pilot, Landing and Takeoff is the hardest part of flying. That's why you want to keep your tenants happy and renting as long as you possibly can.

Running your rental business involves managing finances. The finances you will manage are income and expenses. Basically, you are doing this to offset your rental income (and employment income) with expenses you incur to run your property. Can you guess where I track all my expenses? If you've been reading the previous chapters, you guessed it, Google Spreadsheets.

What's really nice about how I track my expenses is that it automatically enters in all my expenses into my T776(E) Form ready to plug into my Canadian Tax Returns. Wouldn't you love that? Let me show you how.

A T776(E) Form shows your property address, Income and Expenses (hardcopy image shown below). On line 9946 (the last line shown below) it shows whether you made a profit or loss. I structure my Google Spreadsheets the same way. Let me show you how on the next page.

Expenses

Personal use percentage _____ %

		Total expense	Personal portion
Advertising	8521	199 85	
Insurance	8690	2,399 29	
Interest	8710	4,386 48	
Maintenance and repairs	8960	7,640 19	
Management and administration fees	8871	428 81	
Motor vehicle expenses (not including CCA)	9281		
Office expenses	8810	55 03	
Legal, accounting, and other professional fees	8860	114 20	
Property taxes	9180	6,575 60	
Salaries, wages, and benefits (including employer's contributions)	9060		
Travel	9200	3,102 74	
Utilities	9220	298 04	
Other expenses	9270		
Total		25,200 23	9949

Deductible expenses (total expenses **minus** personal portion)			25,200 23 b
Net income (loss) before adjustments (line a **minus** line b)	9369		(15,778 92)
Co-owners - Your share of line 9369 above			(7,889 46) c
Minus: Other expenses of the co-owner	9945		
		Subtotal	(7,889 46)
Plus: Recaptured capital cost allowance (co-owners – enter your share of the amount) (see Chapter 3)	9947		
		Subtotal	(7,889 46)
Minus: Terminal loss (co-owners – enter your share of the amount) (see Chapter 3)	9948		
		Subtotal	(7,889 46)
Minus: Capital cost allowance (from Area A)	9936		
Net income (loss) - If you are a sole proprietor or a co-owner, enter this amount on line 9946			(7,889 46) d
Partnerships - Your share of line d above			(7,889 46)
Plus: GST/HST rebate for partners received in the year	9974		
Minus: Other expenses of the partner	9943		
Your net income (loss) (enter this amount on line 126 of your income tax and benefit return)	9946		(7,889 46)

I have a TAB in my spreadsheet called **"1234 TAX FORM"** where 1234 is the address of my property so I can keep track of several properties. **"1234"** is the Number of my house and so far none of them have the same number.

This TAB is just a summary TAB of data that collects information from other TABs like Expenses. I structure my Expenses in a way that allows me to enter them line by line to describe them, but then I place the amounts into Columns that correlate to the type of expense that the Tax Man is interested in (example – **advertising on line # 8521 of your Canadian tax Form)**.

Where did the $100.00 come from next to the 8521 Tax #? I have a Column in my **"1234 EXPENSES"** TAB that groups just Advertising expenses. I know this is hard to follow so let me show you on the next page what my **"1234 EXPENSES"** Tab looks like.

Income

	# Units	Tax #	Gross Rents	
Address	1		$14,765	
City		8141	$14,765	
Province / State	Other Income	8230		
Postal Code / Zip	Gross income	8299	$14,765 a)	

Expenses

			Total Expense	Personal Portion % 0.00%
Advertising		8521	$100.00	
Insurance		8690	$2,739.00	
Interest		8710	$2,721.79	
Maintenance and Repairs		8960	$5,543.46	
Management and Administration Fees		8871	$0.00	
Motor Vehicle Expenses (not including CCA)		9281	$0.00	
Office Expenses		8810	$26.50	
Legal, Accounting and other Professional Fees		8860	$0.00	
Property Taxes		9180	$3,878.00	
Salaries, Wages, and Benefits (+ employer contributions)		9060	$0.00	
Travel		9200	$0.00	
Utilities		9220	$290.64	
Other Expenses (Capital Cost Base - Property Improvements)	$0.00	9270	$0.00	
	Total		$15,299.39 **9949**	$0

Deductible expenses (total expenses minus personal portion)			$15,299.39 b)
Net income (loss) before adjustments (line a minus line b)		9369	(534.39)
Co-owners - Your share of line 9369 above	100.00%		(534.39) c)
Minus - Other expenses of the co-owner		9945	0.00
		Subtotal	(534.39)
Plus - Recaptured capital cost allowance (co-owners - enter your share of amt)		9947	0.00
		Subtotal	(534.39)
Minus - Terminal Loss (co-owners - enter your share of the amount)		9948	0.00
		Subtotal	(534.39)
Minus - Capital Cost Allowance (from Area A)		9936	0.00
			(534.39) d)
Net income (loss) - If sole proprietor or co-owner, enter this amt on line 9946			(534.39)
Your share of line d) above	100.00%		(534.39)
Minus - Other expenses of the Partner		9943	
Your net income (loss) - Enter this amount on line 126 of your tax return		USD 9946	(534.39)
	Exchange Rate	115.00%	

Notice on the top row I have the TAX Line # **(8521…9270)**. You need to collect and gather all expenses for those categories. It becomes pretty easy when you have all advertising summed up for you under the column with a Tax line number of **8521** (Advertising) - in this case it's $100.00.

This amount gets pulled into the **"1234 TAX FORM"** Tab. How? Easy, on the **"1234 TAX FORM"** TAB just enter an equal sign ("=") into the field you want to pull a value from another cell in another spreadsheet, and go to this spreadsheet and navigate to the $100.00 summary cell at the top and press enter.

From now on, those spreadsheets are linked. That means whenever you enter a new line item into this spreadsheet below for advertising, the total in this spreadsheet will increase, and of course update the other **"1234 TAX FORM"** spreadsheet, because it links to this total and present you with an up to the minute status on whether you are making money or losing it from a Tax perspective.

Of course, you need to collect your income on this property and report that too, but that's pretty easy because those are mostly rent deposits into your bank. Just create another TAB called **"1234 INCOME"**. List the months, summarize the entries, and pull them into your **"1234 TAX FORM"** TAB using the magic equal sign ("=").

There you go. Now you have the killer application for Landlords!

Knowing when you are in the RED or BLACK can help you adjust your Income to Expense ratio from a Tax perspective.

If you make over $100,000 per year in income and want to see a net expense on your balance sheet to help offset or lower your net income tax, this tool will help you.

DATE	DESCRIPTION (1234 SW 21st Pl Cape Coral FL 33914)	PAYMT	8521 Advertising	8690 Insurance	8710 Interest	8960 Maint. & Repairs	8871 Management & Admin Fees	9281 Motor Vehicle Expenses	8810 Office Expenses	8860 Legal, Accounting, Prof Fees	9180 Property Taxes	9060 Salary, Wages, Benefits	9200 Travel	9220 Utilities	9270 Other Expense
	$15,299.39		$100.30	$2,739.00	$2,721.79	$5,543.46	$0.00	$0.00	$26.50	$0.00	$3,878.00	$0.00	$0.00	$298.64	$0.00
2010-01-01	B&M Pool Cleaning					$60.00									
2010-01-01	Green Leaf - Lawn Cutting Service					$75.00									
2010-01-02	AT&T Go Phone	VISA							26.5						
2010-01-05	Hazard Insurance - Olympus Insurance Co.	AUTO		$1,045.00											
2010-01-05	Mortgage Interest	AUTO			$545.51										
2010-01-12	Cape Coral Glass & Mirror	VISA				$92.26									
2010-01-27	Cape Coral Glass & Mirror	VISA				$439.00									
2010-02-01	B&M Pool Cleaning					$60.00									
2010-02-01	Green Leaf - Lawn Cutting Service					$75.00									
2010-02-04	R&R Sprinklers Inc.	153				$101.00									
2010-02-05	Mortgage Interest	AUTO			$544.94										
2010-03-01	B&M Pool Cleaning					$60.00									
2010-03-01	Green Leaf - Lawn Cutting Service					$75.00									
2010-03-05	Mortgage Interest	AUTO			$544.36										
2010-04-01	B&M Pool Cleaning					$60.00									
2010-04-01	Green Leaf - Lawn Cutting Service					$75.00									
2010-04-05	Mortgage Interest	AUTO			$543.78										
2010-05-01	B&M Pool Cleaning					$60.00									
2010-05-01	Green Leaf - Lawn Cutting Service					$75.00									
2010-05-05	Mortgage Interest	AUTO			$543.20										
2010-06-01	B&M Pool Cleaning					$60.00									
2010-06-01	Green Leaf - Lawn Cutting Service					$75.00									
2010-06-05	Mortgage Interest	AUTO													
2010-06-11	Flood Insurance - ASI - American Standard Insurance	AUTO		$809.00											
2010-06-11	Olympus Home Owners Insurance	AUTO		$885.00											
2010-07-01	B&M Pool Cleaning					$60.00									
2010-07-01	Green Leaf - Lawn Cutting Service					$75.00									
2010-07-05	Mortgage Interest	AUTO													
2010-08-01	B&M Pool Cleaning					$60.00									
2010-08-01	Green Leaf - Lawn Cutting Service					$75.00									
2010-08-05	Mortgage Interest	AUTO													
2010-09-01	B&M Pool Cleaning					$60.00									
2010-09-01	Green Leaf - Lawn Cutting Service					$75.00									
2010-09-05	Mortgage Interest	AUTO													
2010-10-01	B&M Pool Cleaning					$60.00									
2010-10-01	Green Leaf - Lawn Cutting Service					$75.00									
2010-10-05	Mortgage Interest	AUTO													
2010-11-01	B&M Pool Cleaning					$60.00									
2010-11-01	Green Leaf - Lawn Cutting Service					$75.00									
2010-11-01	Lee County Property Tax	AUTO									$3,878.00				
2010-11-05	Mortgage Interest	AUTO													
2010-12-01	B&M Pool Cleaning					$60.00									
2010-12-01	Green Leaf - Lawn Cutting Service					$75.00									

Another spreadsheet you should manage is your asset or appliance list. I know it seems tedious but it becomes easier to find information when you need to call for service. I highly recommend buying appliances with a 4 year warranty which provides you with peace of mind and replacement insurance.

If your tenant ever calls you, all you do is call Lowes or Home Depot or wherever you bought your appliances from and they'll be at your property to fix it for free. The cost is usually $100 for 4 years and has paid back in dividends for me.

Again, now that you're a Google DOCS Spreadsheet wizard, I know you are ready to create this new masterpiece. No more fumbling for paperwork when you call for service. You know the serial # and the model # and away you go.

	Purchased at	Year	Make	Model	Serial #	SKU	Price	Parts Cost	Delivery	Installation	Tax	Total	Warranty $	With Warranty	Warranty #	Warr Term (Yrs)	Expires
4231																	
Fridge	Home Depot	9/18/2009	Maytag	MSD2542VEW00	HRW3562051		$759.10	$9.99	$65.00		$46.15	$880.24	$99.95	$980.19	333345422	4	9/17/2014
Dishwasher [1]	Home Depot	8/11/2008	Maytag	MDB8601AWW			$549.00	$29.98	$65.00	$80.00		$723.98	$99.95	$823.93		4	8/10/2013
Stove	Lowes	6/13/2010	Maytag	MER7765			$649.00	$19.47				$668.47	$99.97	$768.44	0059204310164102648	4	6/12/2015
Microwave	Original	2003										$0.00		$0			
Washer	Original	2003										$0.00		$0			
Dryer	Original	2003										$0.00		$0			
														$2572.56			
1529																	
Fridge	Lowes	8/2/2009	Whirpool	ED5LVAXWB		127	$1,078.20				$305.92	$1,384.12		$1384.12	0059201309214125104	4	8/1/2014
Dishwasher [1]	Lowes	8/2/2009	Frigidaire	FDB4050LHB		312545	$403.20	$19.45				$422.65	$159.97	$582.62	0059201309214125104	4	8/1/2014
Stove	Lowes	8/2/2009	Whirpool	GY397LXJB		293959	$1,213.20	$15.45				$1,228.65		$1228.65	0059201309214125104	4	8/1/2014
Microwave	Lowes	8/2/2009	Whirpool	WMH2175XVB		313022	$250.20					$250.20	$159.97	$410.17	0059201309214125104	4	8/1/2014
Washer	Lowes	8/2/2009	BOSCH	WFMC5301U		278392	$808.20					$808.20	$159.97	$968.17	0059201309214125104	4	8/1/2014
Dryer	Lowes	8/2/2009	BOSCH	WTMC5321US		31833	$808.20	$22.83				$831.03	$159.97	$991	0059201309214125104	4	8/1/2014
														$5564.73			
5337																	
Fridge	Lowes	11/2/2010	Whirpool	ED5LVAXWQ		138	$989.00		Included		$59.34	$1,048.34	$90.00	$1138.34	0236101510301150830	4	11/1/2015
Dishwasher [1]	Original																
Stove	Lowes	11/2/2010	Frigidaire	LGEF3033KW		24857	$699.00	$21.97		Included	$43.26	$784.23	$90.00	$854.23	0236101510301150830	4	11/1/2015
Microwave	None																
Washer	Good Deals	7/6/2009	Whirpool	WFW8400TW			$600.00					$600.00	$129.99	$729.99		5	7/5/2015
Dryer	Good Deals	7/6/2009	Whirpool	WED830CSW			$599.00	$30.00	$55.00		$92.64	$776.64	$129.99	$906.63		5	7/5/2015
														$3,629.19			

I know by now that you are starting to become your own wizard at this stuff, especially if you've been practicing what I told you.

If not, don't worry, you will become a Wizard, because once you start, it becomes highly contagious.

Renting your Vacation Property

Renting a vacation property is very different than renting to annual renters. My strategy is to rent to annual tenants first to get steady income then one day, when they move out, and when the time is right, I will convert the home into a vacation rental.

When turning your property into a vacation rental, you need to spend some upfront cash. You will need some upfront investment to furnish it, buy and install TV screens, a Computer, an internet and cable / satellite connection and probably invest into a pool heater if you don't already have one. Most people will want to rent during the winter months. Florida winters are nowhere near as cold as Canadian winters but swimming is not as enjoyable unless you have a heated pool and many will ask for it.

If you want to do some market research on what your property would fetch as a vacation rental, start looking at some websites, like http://www.vacationrental.com or http://www.vrbo.com. In fact, you could even post an advertisement into www.vacationrental.com for free to see what type of calls you get. If you get enough interest from the public looking for a winter escape and can get enough bookings during the winter months, then you could start planning to turn it into a vacation retreat. VRBO will cost you about $250 per year, but it has a large community of consumers looking for rentals on an international scale. Remember, lots of Europeans will go to Florida instead of the Mediterranean mostly because of the value for the Euro they get.

The reason why many vacationers choose vacation rentals is because they know they can get a private pool, a full kitchen with all amenities, usually 3 bedrooms with 2+ bathrooms that can accommodate 6-8 people. It's basically better value for the dollar. The average home rental per month in Florida is around $3,000 USD per month depending on views and amenities. If you wanted to rent the property as an annual rental you would normally get about $1,000 / month. Therefore, renting it as a vacation rental means you can make your annual earnings in one third of the time.

You can also use it yourself or continue renting it on a weekly basis for families wanting a summer escape to the beach when kids are off during the summer.

Owning a vacation rental can be a money machine. It can fund the things you most like to do at retirement. One of those retirement things could be going down to Florida to use that money to golf, swim or snorkel at the beach, go boating, marlin fishing, shop at the outlets, eat at great seafood restaurants, see dolphins swimming near the shores.

Did I mention you wouldn't have to pay for any Hotel?

Rental Type	Rental Period	Rent/Month	Rent Collected During Period	Extra Income (off peak season)
Annual	Jan-Dec (12 months)	$1,000	$12,000	N/A
Vacation	Dec-Mar (4 months)	$3,000	$12,000	$2,000/month or $800/week

10 Things you should know in getting started

1. **Get a pre-approved ELOC (Equity Line of Credit)**

An ELOC (Equity Line of Credit) will provide you with the ability to perform financial bridging, should you need it. Remember that paying cash for a house is a more solid offer than a deal that is based on financing. Pre-approved mortgages with banks are fine for standard home purchase. Applying for home loan to purchase a house will take between 45-60 days to process. Buying short sales and foreclosures don't always have predictable time frames. For a short sale, your offer could sit for months before getting an approval from the seller (home owner) and the lender (bank that holds the mortgage with seller). Having an ELOC can sometimes rescue you by allowing you to buy the house in cash, then after you on title to it, you could then apply for financing on the home. In order to open an ELOC, you will need to incur the legal fees (approximately $500) to draw up the appraisal and paperwork. The equity line will be limited to 75% of the current value of your existing home and the amount you have already paid off on it. If you have a house appraised at $600,000 and you only owe $250,000 on it, then you'll have $200,000 of equity you could borrow on it (75% of $600,000 = $450,000 less $250,000 still owed leaves $200,000 of available equity).

2. **Find yourself a great Real Estate Agent**

This can make or break your experience. Keep looking until you find the right agent to represent you. You could visit Trulia to start looking to see what agents and people are discussing online. However, the best way is to actually fly down to where you want to buy and have a few agents lined up to call to meet them in person and to see what they are like to work with. They can tell you about the area and their experience. Go look at homes with them after you agree on the criteria for the type of property you are interested in. Find out if your agent has worked with Canadians before or other Foreign Nationals. Also find out if your agent is willing to email you pictures of homes when you are searching from Canada.

3. **Take a trip – Go Scout out your Area**

It's important to see the neighborhood, the beaches, the golf courses, the restaurants and the type of homes you want to purchase. Make it an enjoyable trip for yourself. Don't make it all business or all relaxation. A good balance will keep you motivated and excited about buying in the area you want to invest in. Make it a week-long trip and try to get some beach days and golf days in. While you are down there, get yourself some USA bank accounts and credit cards, see next section.

4. **Get a USA Bank Chequing account**

This is something you are going to need. A chequing account will be needed to pay fees, bills, utilities, surveys, and for professional services to fix things up once you take ownership of your property. You will also need this account to accept your incoming rent cheques from tenants once you start renting out your place. You will also need a USA account to receive USA funds from your Canadian banks as you wire money across or to receive foreign exchange funds from your XE Trade account. To get a USA bank account, you need to appear in person with your passport to verify and confirm you are who you say you are. No USA bank accounts can be setup online or over the web or phone because of the Patriot Act and money laundering regulations.

5. **Get a USA Bank Credit Card**

This credit card will be needed if you want to order anything online from Canada but need it shipped to a USA address. For example, you cannot order an Appliance form a Home Depot USA site and enter in a Canadian credit card and have your stove shipped to a USA address. It just doesn't work as the credit card needs to have a ZIP CODE associated with it with a valid USA mailing address. Besides providing convenience in having a credit card to purchase things online, using your credit card will also start establishing your credit score.

6. Get pre-approved by a USA Bank for a Mortgage

Getting a pre-approval will help you understand how much the bank is willing to lend you and at what interest rate. The interest rate will be locked in for a period of time, usually 90 days, so if rates go up, you'll still be able to use the rate you were quoted.

7. Get an XE Trade Account (https://fx2.xe.com/fxlogin/)

An XE Trade account allows you to convert Canadian funds into American. Why not do this at your bank? The reason is because they'll charge you a couple of percent more for doing the exchange. With currency exchange there's always a bid and an ask price. You normally get charged the spread (the difference between the bid and ask) plus a fee for doing the exchange. The bank adds another 1-2% on top of that. XE Trade only charges a fraction of that. Register for an account and have it ready when you need it. It doesn't cost you anything. You will need to fax into them a Notary signed by your Dentist or someone that can sign a copy of your passport to vouch for you. On a $225,000 transaction I saved about $4,500 versus going with a big Canadian bank. That's money I could use.

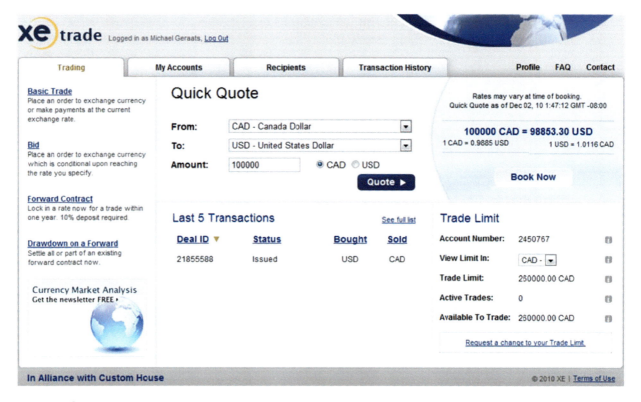

8. Get all your Google Accounts setup

Although I explained why you need these accounts previously in the book you should start setting them up.

9. Get onto the Real Estate search sites and setup your Alerts for property

Go to the sites explained in the next section entitled "Search Tools of the Trade" on page 86 and start setting up your alerts to be emailed reports on homes that come available within your price range, location, square footage, number of bedrooms, with pool or not, Gulf access or whatever criteria appeals to you.

10. **Get ready for the ride of your life**

You are going to enjoy this, so have fun with it. I honestly felt this was a valid thing you needed to know.

Search Tools of the Trade

Below are tools I used in my journey to find properties that were thousands of miles away but give me enough data to help me make my decisions.

ZILLOW

Zillow provides an estimate of home value based by recent sales activity in various regions. It also provides information on the neighborhood like nearby schools, other homes that sold in the area and at what price. It's a very visual type of website showing graphs of home sales in the area. As you can see, the graph shows the home in relation to the area and the entire zip code. Home owners can "claim" their home on Zillow and give the real details on what was done to the property plus add pictures. I have to my properties, and it's a good idea because it keeps it real.

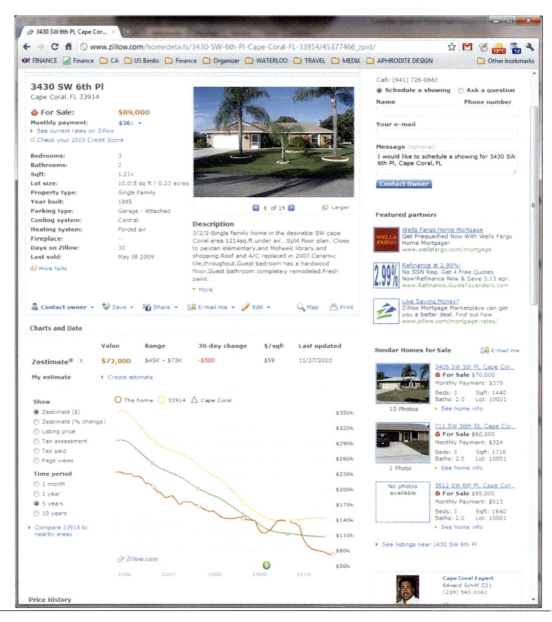

ZIPREALTY

ZipRealty has a unique and powerful website. The best thing about ZipRealty is that you can get email alerts for homes you search on. When you create a search for a type of home you can specify that you want to be notified by email on homes that show up matching your search criteria.

ZipRealty also promises to return a portion of the real estate agent's commission to you if you decide to purchase through one of their real estate agents. As shown below this amount would be $3,900 cash back to you should you decide to purchase.

You can click on the **Maps** Tab next to the **Home Detail** tab to see where the house is on the map. You can also show local schools in the area and how they rank state wide which will be important to any tenants you want to rent to.

If you like the house, then just click on the Save Home Orange button below and it will hold this property in your search basket to review later with other homes that you like. Now you are starting to create a selection of homes to share with your real estate agent that could schedule home showings with you when you decide to go down.

Also if you like this type of home, size, area, amenities and price, the tool automatically builds a **Similar Homes You May Like** list located below.

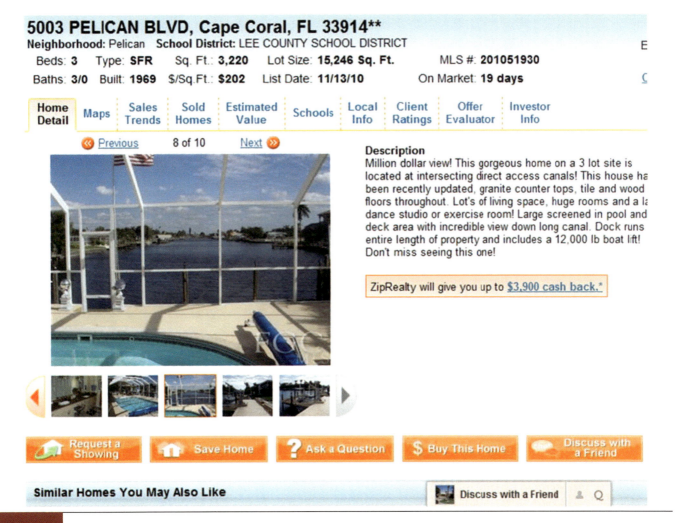

5003 PELICAN BLVD, Cape Coral, FL 33914**

Neighborhood: Pelican   School District: LEE COUNTY SCHOOL DISTRICT

Beds: **3**   Type: **SFR**   Sq. Ft.: **3,220**   Lot Size: **15,246 Sq. Ft.**   MLS #: **201051930**

Baths: **3/0**   Built: **1969** $/Sq.Ft.: **$202**   List Date: **11/13/10**   On Market: **19 days**

| Home Detail | Maps | Sales Trends | Sold Homes | Estimated Value | Schools | Local Info | Client Ratings | Offer Evaluator | Investor Info |

« Previous   8 of 10   Next »

Description
Million dollar view! This gorgeous home on a 3 lot site is located at intersecting direct access canals! This house ha been recently updated, granite counter tops, tile and wood floors throughout. Lot's of living space, huge rooms and a la dance studio or exercise room! Large screened in pool and deck area with incredible view down long canal. Dock runs entire length of property and includes a 12,000 lb boat lift! Don't miss seeing this one!

ZipRealty will give you up to $3,900 cash back.*

Request a Showing   Save Home   Ask a Question   Buy This Home   Discuss with a Friend

Similar Homes You May Also Like   Discuss with a Friend

A really nice feature of this search tool is that it has an Interactive Map search tool feature that allows you to seach based on map location. This is similar to ZILLOW. Listings with pictures are shown with a Camera icon. You can also narrow your search to look for just **Short Sales**, or **Foreclosures**, or homes that are in need of renovation called **Fixer Uppers**.

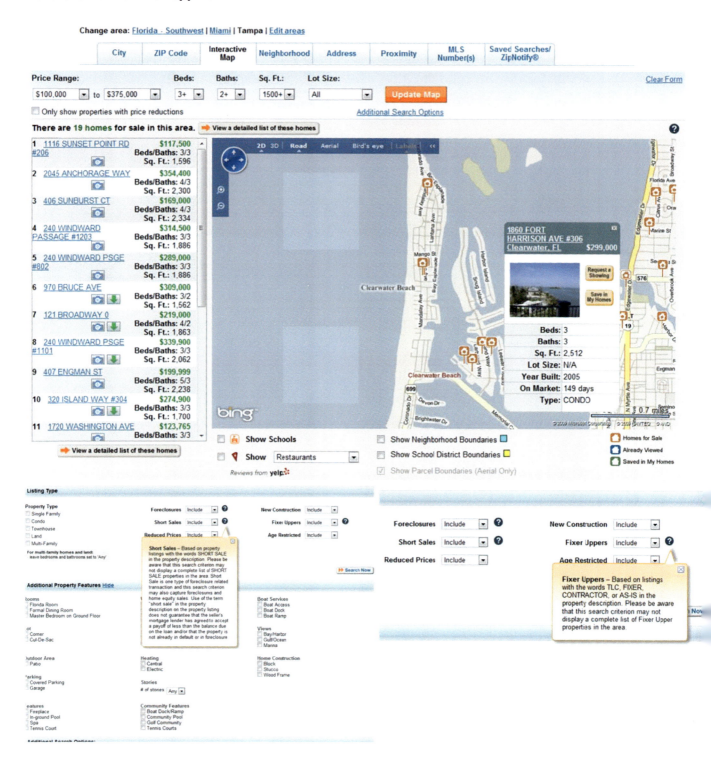

LISTINGBOOK

Listingbook provides good information about area home values, recent sales activity in various regions and has good pictures and image processing tools. It can even provide a Morning report sent to you daily after you enter you home criteria. The thing I like best about this tool is that you can specify a geographic area to focus on and only send you properties up for sale within that geographic area.

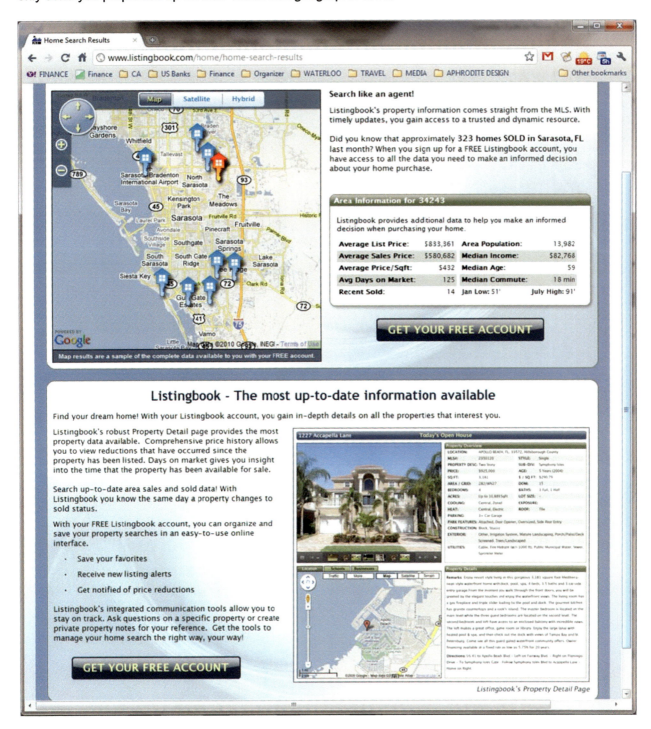

Build the search area by choosing ANY COMBINATION (max 25) of Standard Areas, Sub-Divisions, Condos/Townhomes/Villas and/or Map Search selections

Standard Areas | Sub-Divisions | Condos/Townhomes/Villas | **Map Search**

Update Search Areas

Search Areas (24 slots available)

Map Selection: 7.88 sq miles around <26.552, -82.001>

| Frontpage | Home Finder | My Favorites | Agent Picks | Quick Search | Calendar | Mess |

■ Home Finder Results

One Line | Thumbnail | Comparison | Portfolio | **Map** |

Home Finder Results: 39 properties

Page 1 ▾ 🖶 Print

🔍 Home Finder Criteria

Order by:
Last Change Date ▾

Residential | Lots & Land | Rental

🟨 New or Changed 🟦 Previously Reported 👓 Viewed
🟩 Perfect Match 🅰 ctive 🅿 ending AB
🅰 ctive Contingent Short Sale 🆗 Open House
⭐ Featured Listing

🔖 Add Selected to My Favorites
🔖 Reject Selected Properties
🔭 View Selected Properties Only

1. ☐ 🅰 **5232 SW 18th Ave**
   View on map
2. ☐ 🅰 **2127 SW 49th St**
   View on map
3. ☐ 🅰 **223 Santa Monica Ct**
   View on map
4. ☐ 🅰 **5208 SW 2nd Pl**
   View on map
5. ☐ 🅰 **1428 SW 49th Ter**
   View on map
6. ☐ 🅰 **5508 SW 5th Ave**
   View on map
7. ☐ 🅰 **5334 Cocoa Ct**
   View on map
8. ☐ 🅰 **2225 SW 50th St**
   View on map
9. ☐ 🅰 **5020 Saxony Ct**
   View on map
10. ☐ 🅰 **4819 SW 2nd Pl**
    View on map
11. ☐ 🅰 **5031 SW 9th Pl**
    View on map
12. ☐ 🅰 **4927 SW 2nd Pl**
    View on map

🅰 Agent Note 🅱 Buyer Note
Rejected Properties: Show ▾

🔖 Add Selected to My Favorites
🔖 Reject Selected Properties
🔭 View Selected Properties Only

[<< Last Page]   1 2 3 4   [**Next Page >>**]

NAPLES GULF LIVING

LISTINGBOOK

NaplesGulfLiving was born out of Naples through Prudential Florida Realty but it can cover most of the Southern Florida. This search tool has superior image hovering technology when you mouse over the photo it expands automatically and can save you many clicks. I used it a lot to find Miami Condos and actually made a special Condo shopping trip out of it.

Virtual tours are offered when you see the button below. It also includes a walk score, telling you what's within walking distance, like restaurants, coffee shop, bars etc.

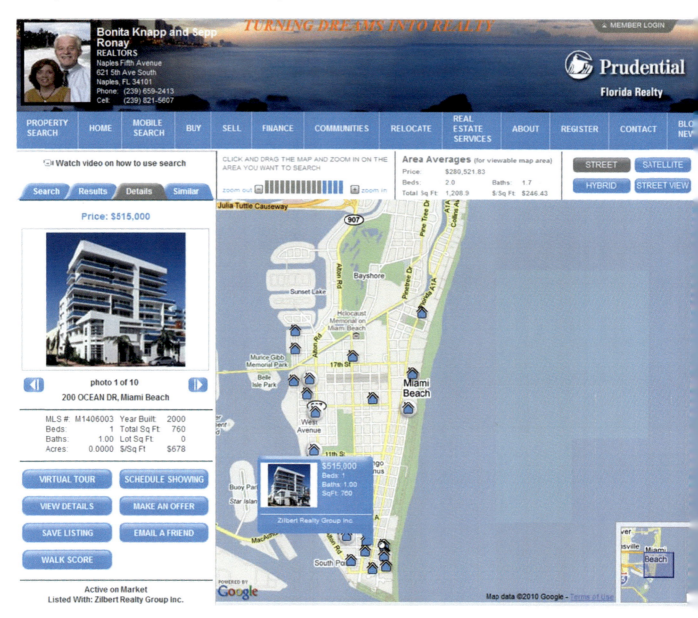

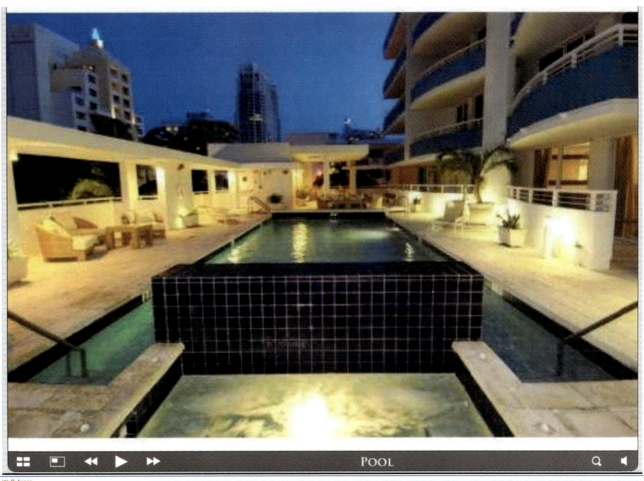

POOL

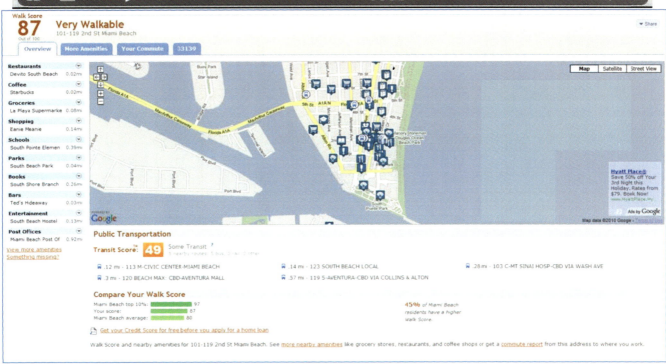

TRULIA

TRULIA

Trulia is a great site to ask local realtors about areas, or homes. You will get responses from realtors or see questions from other interested investors.

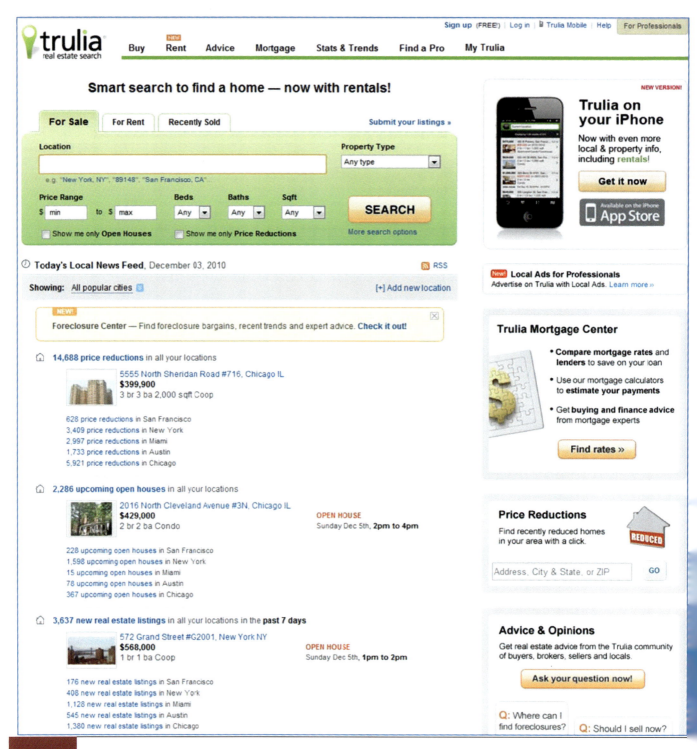

Getting Down to Florida

There are a few tips I wanted to share with you on how to get down and make the best use of your money when going down to Florida on your property search or your annual visitation to see properties you have invested in.

If you are going down to search for properties and will be calling real estate agents to show you places or trades people to help you fix up your investment, you will need a local cell phone. You can buy phones for $7.99 with a pre-paid SIM card that can be refilled using a credit card.

Get a phone number that has a local Florida area code. You can order a SIM card from AT&T or T-Mobile or Verizon Wireless and then insert that SIM into your own cell phone. I order the AT&T GO Phone which ships to you and can be activated for use within Florida. The cost per minute is usually .10 cents and is free if the real estate agent you are calling is also an AT&T customer.

http://www.wireless.att.com/cell-phone-service/cell-phones/prepaid-phones.jsp

Another area to save money is air travel. I use AirTrans (now SouthWest Airlines), JetBlue, and DirectAir which all fly out of Buffalo and Niagara Airports. If you are in Western Canada WestJet may be a good option. Air Canada is a good choice also if you are flying to Miami and can sometimes have competitive fares. I usually pay $250 return all taxes and fees included using AirTran/Southwest and DirectAir.

DirectAir has direct flights – non-stop to West Palm Beach on the East coast (90 minutes North of Miami) or Punta Gorda on the West Coast (about 45 minutes North of Fort Myers). You can also fly direct to Orlando with Air Trans (SouthWest Airlines) on some flights.

Use FLY.com to help you find the best option.

About the Author

You might have expected this section to be about my credentials in investing, or real estate and finance. However, if you read my introductory chapter you already know I've made plenty of investment mistakes. The truth is that I learned from my bad investment practices over several years and know when there's a good time to jump in. Now is that time.

In 1989 I violated the 3 most basic rules of successful real estate investing when I purchased my first income property. I bought high and sold low, I chose the worst location in Toronto and I picked a Real Estate agent that I should have fired long before getting to the closing stage. This time is different. I know that I'm not buying high because we are in the trough (and may be for a while – my prediction is about 6 years). Our location in Florida was researched over the course of a year and we chose carefully where we would be happy to live ourselves and know where tenants are looking to work and live. Finally, our agent Dawn Grummel, is one of the finest we know in the industry and took the time to service our needs with limitless patience.

In fact, my true fortune in life was meeting my wife Catherine, at a dance club about 25 years ago. We married on Valentine's Day in 1987 and raised two amazing children, Sabrina and Cameron. Catherine was my inspiration for writing this book as she agreed to go on this journey with me. She not only agreed to take this financial risk but provided support and guidance every step of the way. Catherine was my voice of reason when I was an emotional roller coaster bringing her properties that I saw for sale surfing the internet at 5:00am. I couldn't wait for her to wake-up so that I could bring her my morning filtered search results. Of course, that required bringing her English Breakfast tea before I gained entry to her counsel.

It was difficult convincing Catherine that we could buy a home over the internet without having to go see it in person. However, she agreed we could do it if we knew exactly what we were looking for and with the help of a very admirable real estate agent taking pictures of those homes and sending them to us for closer inspection.

Since I don't have any of the above mentioned credentials in Real Estate or Finance, was also a reason why I wrote this book. It hopefully shows you that you don't need anything other than a desire to explore this market and to look after your retirement years. We could all use a helping hand when it comes to saving for our retirement with so many wealth creation options disappearing and where our government is less able to look after us.

I hope this book was informative, inspiring and thought provoking to help you on your journey to wealth creation. I also hope you realize that there are a lot of free tools and vehicles out there if you look long and hard enough. Most people don't have the time and hopefully this book consolidates it for you.

I have thoroughly enjoyed this time of my life by exploring and searching for properties into the panhandle. I have not only invested for my generation but also for our children. I hope you have even half the fun and excitement I had and wish you the best luck in your search and hope you refer your friends to my book as their guide. It will certainly save you a lot of time answering all the questions that need to be answered. You'll need that time to search for your second property.

By the way, if you are looking in the South Gulf Coast region of Florida, like Cape Coral, Fort Myers, Estero, Bonita Springs, Naples, I encourage you to call my Real Estate Agent, Dawn Grummel from Century 21 Birchwood Realty. Tell her I sent you by reading my book.

Dawn was the reason why I've invested in Florida. She brings her warm Florida charm to work every single day and makes looking for properties an exciting and enjoyable experience and we owe much of our success to her. Just Google her name and you will find her or call her directly at 239-246-9590.

CPSIA information can be obtained
at www.ICGtesting.com
Printed in the USA
276002LV00011B